The Tuition Dilemma

THE
TUITION
DILEMMA

Assessing New Ways to Pay for College

Arthur M. Hauptman

The Brookings Institution
Washington, D.C.

Copyright © 1990 by
THE BROOKINGS INSTITUTION
1775 Massachusetts Avenue., N.W., Washington, D.C. 20036

Library of Congress Cataloging-in-Publication data:

Hauptman, Arthur M.
    The tuition dilemma : assessing new ways to pay for
college / Arthur M. Hauptman.
        p. cm.
    ISBN 0-8157-3502-2 (alk. paper)—ISBN 0-8157-3501-4
(pbk. : alk. paper)
        1. College costs—United States. 2. Universities and
colleges—United States—Finance. 3. Student aid—United
States. I. Title.
LB2342.H385 1990   89-78071
378.3'0973—dc20   CIP

9 8 7 6 5 4 3 2 1

The paper used in this publication meets the minimum
requirements of the American National Standard for
Information Sciences—Permanence of Paper for Printed
Library Materials, ANSI Z39.48-1984.

Set in Linotron Century Schoolbook
Composition by Monotype Composition Co.
  Baltimore, Maryland
Printing by R.R. Donnelley and Sons Co.
  Harrisonburg, Virginia
Book Design by Ken Sabol
Cover Design by Linda McKnight

THE BROOKINGS INSTITUTION

The Brookings Institution is an independent organization devoted to nonpartisan research, education, and publication in economics, government, foreign policy, and the social sciences generally. Its principal purposes are to aid in the development of sound public policies and to promote public understanding of issues of national importance.

The Institution was founded on December 8, 1927, to merge the activities of the Institute for Government Research, founded in 1916, the Institute of Economics, founded in 1922, and the Robert Brookings Graduate School of Economics and Government, founded in 1924.

The Board of Trustees is responsible for the general administration of the Institution, while the immediate direction of the policies, program, and staff is vested in the President, assisted by an advisory committee of the officers and staff. The by-laws of the Institution state: "It is the function of the Trustees to make possible the conduct of scientific research, and publication, under the most favorable conditions, and to safeguard the independence of the research staff in the pursuit of their studies and in the publication of the results of such studies. It is not a part of their function to determine, control, or influence the conduct of particular investigations or the conclusions reached."

The President bears final responsibility for the decision to publish a manuscript as a Brookings book. In reaching his judgment on the competence, accuracy, and objectivity of each study, the President is advised by the director of the appropriate research program and weighs the views of a panel of expert outside readers who report to him in confidence on the quality of the work. Publication of a work signifies that it is deemed a competent treatment worthy of public consideration but does not imply endorsement of conclusions or recommendations.

The Institution maintains its position of neutrality on issues of public policy in order to safeguard the intellectual freedom of the staff. Hence interpretations or conclusions in Brookings publications should be understood to be solely those of the authors and should not be attributed to the Institution, to its trustees, officers, or other staff members, or to the organizations that support its research.

Foreword

In the 1980s students and their families became increasingly concerned about how they were going to pay for college. With tuitions increasing twice as fast as inflation, fewer families could rely on their incomes to pay for rising college charges. Government student aid programs also failed to expand fast enough to keep pace with increases in the cost of attending college. Moreover, the declining size of the traditional college-age group, some apparent erosion in the belief that parents should pay for their children's college education, and a lack of progress in increasing the participation of low-income and minority students raised disturbing questions about the future financing of American higher education.

In response to these trends, federal and state governments, colleges and universities, and various groups in the private sector have developed innovative financing plans. This book is designed to help policymakers and others through the maze of options that exist. The author examines the trends in financing and participation that have stimulated the growing demand for alternative financing plans; the issues raised by the new proposals for tuition prepayment, guarantees, and savings; some methods for evaluating these proposals; and the appropriate objectives of public policy in the realm of financing higher education.

The analysis presented here is an outgrowth of a policy forum held at the Brookings Institution in June 1988. The book is not, however, a research publication of the Institution and has not been subjected to the formal review and verification procedures established for such publications.

Arthur M. Hauptman is an independent consultant specializing in higher education financing and federal budget issues. He is grateful to those who helped in the development of this book. Alice M. Rivlin cochaired the policy forum at Brookings and provided general direction for the project. James D. Carroll coordinated the activities of the forum. Jamie Merisotis assisted with many aspects of the project, particularly by researching new ways of paying for college and by writing a summary of the proceedings of the forum. In addition, a number of people provided useful comments on early drafts, including Peter Keitel, David Longanecker, Francis McLaughlin, Maureen McLaughlin, Michael McPherson, and Robert Reischauer. Those who participated in the policy forum also played a critical role. Many of the ideas discussed there are reflected in the book. Venka Macintyre edited the manuscript, and Max Franke prepared the index.

Brookings is grateful to the Teagle Foundation for providing financial assistance for this project.

The views expressed here are those of the author and should not be attributed to the foundation or to the trustees, officers, or staff members of the Brookings Institution.

BRUCE K. MACLAURY
President

January 1990
Washington, D.C.

Contents

The Tuition Dilemma

Chapter One

Trends in Higher Education Financing and Participation

Higher education in the United States has grown enormously since the end of the Second World War. College and university enrollments have increased nearly fourfold since 1950, and expenditures and revenues have multiplied nearly tenfold in constant dollars. This rapid expansion can be traced to a number of important trends in financing and participation from the end of the war through the 1970s:

—Although annual tuition increases averaged a percentage point or two higher than inflation, increases in family income kept college affordable for most students and their families.

—Student aid programs were established and expanded to encourage the attendance of students who otherwise would not have enrolled. Government funding of higher education, through state support of public institutions as well as federal and state student aid programs, increased sharply to finance this expansion.

—The baby boom, which produced record numbers of students in the traditional college-age group of eighteen- to twenty-four-year-olds, swelled college enrollments. In addition, opportunities were expanded for minorities and students from other groups who traditionally were underrepresented in higher education.

In the 1980s, however, there were significant and troubling shifts in these earlier trends. Tuitions and other college charges increased much more rapidly than inflation or family incomes, while the growth in state institutional support and student aid availability slowed, although it still increased in real terms. There was much publicity over the marked shift from grants to

1

loans as the primary form of aid; loan usage increased sharply, whereas funding for grants grew only modestly in real terms. The enrollment boom of the 1960s and early 1970s was followed by a decline in the size of the traditional college-age group and a leveling in the number of college students. Enrollments would have fallen if the number of older, nontraditional college students had not grown. Also, the college participation rates of minorities and low-income students appear to have reached a plateau or decreased, after a period of much progress. Policymakers need to take a close look at these shifts in financing patterns and participation trends before they can adequately assess the relative merits of the new options for financing a college education.

The Rapid Growth in College Charges

Since 1980 the price of a college education—as measured by tuition, fees, room and board, and other charges—increased much faster than the costs of a range of other goods and services. Tuition alone, at both private and public institutions, increased almost twice as fast as inflation. The average annual increase in college tuitions from 1980 to 1987 was about 10 percent, whereas the price index for food and new cars each rose 4 percent a year, and the median price of a new house grew at 7 percent. Even the health care industry, long an especially inflationary sector, lagged behind: the average annual increase in the medical care component of the consumer price index (CPI) was about 8 percent.[1]

Increases in college charges in the 1980s also far outstripped the growth in family incomes. From 1980 to 1987 the median family income increased by nearly 50 percent, whereas tuitions rose almost 90 percent. In real terms, median family income grew by about 6 percent during this period, while the inflation-adjusted increase in tuitions was in excess of 30 percent. Much attention

1. Consumer prices are from U.S. Department of Labor, Bureau of Labor Statistics. Tuition figures are from U. S. Department of Education, *Digest of Education Statistics,* various years.

has been paid to this fact as an indication of the growing disparity between college costs and the family resources available to pay for them.[2]

In recent years a number of analysts have questioned whether median family income is an accurate measure of the changing financial strength of American families, principally because it may not reflect the impact of the shrinkage in the average size of families on buying power. As a result, the Congressional Budget Office (CBO) adjusted median family income to reflect the changing average size of families, as well as changes over time in how the consumer price index is measured.[3] With these refinements, the CBO index of adjusted family income rose by 7 percent between 1980 and 1986, whereas inflation-adjusted college tuitions rose by about 30 percent. Still another measure of income is disposable personal income per capita, which reflects the effects of changing tax burdens as well as changes in family size. From 1980 through 1986 disposable personal income per capita grew by about 15 percent in real terms, again well behind tuitions.

Even these national measures of income may not fully reflect the extent to which rising college charges are affecting families that are trying to pay for college. Figures are available on median family income and the CBO-adjusted family income based on the age of the head of household. In families with heads between the ages of thirty-five and fifty-four (which is the group that most traditional college-age children would come from), incomes increased by slightly more than 10 percent in real terms between 1980 and 1986, which, though faster than the average for all ages, is still far behind tuitions. For the increasing proportion of college students who are not of traditional college age or financially dependent on their parents, however, an age-adjusted measure of income may not accurately reflect the current realities of college enrollments and economies.

2. Information on median family income is from U.S. Bureau of the Census, *Current Population Reports,* series P-60, various years.
3. Congressional Budget Office, *Trends in Family Income, 1970–1986* (1988).

Thus college tuitions in the 1980s jumped ahead of inflation or income by virtually any measure. This situation helps to explain the frantic search for new ways to finance college costs. It is not unlike the search for innovative financing alternatives in the housing industry that began in the 1970s, when housing prices climbed to the point where many families could no longer finance their housing needs through traditional means.

In the 1970s, however, tuitions and other charges grew more slowly than the general rate of inflation and incomes. When measured from 1970 through 1987, tuition increases fall in the middle of the pack in comparison with other goods and services, rising slightly faster than the general rate of inflation. From 1970 to 1987 tuitions grew about one percentage point a year faster than median family income, but one-half percentage point slower than the annual increase in disposable personal income per capita.

When tuition increases are compared with the price of housing over time, four years of tuition at a public institution was roughly 5 percent of the median price of a new house in 1965, and the average tuition at a private institution was about 23 percent of the median price of a new house. In the intervening years, public tuitions as a proportion of housing prices have stayed fairly constant. In contrast, private tuitions rose to 29 percent of housing prices in 1970, fell to 22 percent by 1980, and then climbed back to 27 percent by 1987.

It is also useful to compare tuition increases with changes in the value of stocks and bonds and other investments, which serve as a means for parents to save for their children's education. From 1980 to 1987 the pretax return on common stocks was one-half greater than the increase in tuitions, whereas stock returns were about one-third greater than tuition increases in the 1970s. The total pretax return on the best-rated corporate bonds lagged behind tuition growth in the 1970s, but was more than twice as large in the 1980s; between 1970 and 1987 the total return on bonds slightly outpaced the increase in tuitions. Municipal bond yields have been slightly lower than tuition increases since 1970, with a noticeable lag occurring in the late 1970s. The average yields on Treasury bills by and large kept pace with tuition increases throughout the 1970s and 1980s.[4]

However, the after-tax return on these investments—with the possible exception of stocks—has not kept up with tuition increases since 1970. Consequently, families are looking for new investment vehicles that capitalize on tax benefits and pooling efforts that allow savings for college to grow at least as fast as future increases in college charges.

Shifts in Financing Patterns

Historically, higher education in the United States has been financed in three principal ways: through the contributions of parents and students; through state appropriations to public sector institutions; and through voluntary gifts from alumni and others, especially to institutions in the private sector. Although the support provided by governments and the voluntary sector is sizable, families and students pay a much larger share of what it costs to provide a college education than do their counterparts in other industrialized nations. Despite this burden, or perhaps because of it, a far higher proportion of Americans continue their education beyond high school than people in other countries. Today more than half of all American high school graduates can be expected to enroll in a postsecondary educational program at some time or other.

State appropriations for public institutions, which have grown in current dollars from $6 billion in 1970 to almost $20 billion in 1980 to over $32 billion in 1987, are the principal form of government funding for higher education. With these state funds at their disposal, public institutions are able to charge roughly one-fifth or less of what it costs them to provide a college education. Large increases in this source of funding helped to fuel the expansion in enrollments and facilities at public institutions from 1950 through the mid-1970s; since then, growth in the funding source and in enrollments has slowed. In real terms, state support

4. Stock and bond yields are from Ibbotson Associates, *Stocks, Bonds, Bills, and Inflation*, 1987 Yearbook (Chicago, 1989).

of higher education grew by 6 percent a year in the first half of the 1970s, dropped to 2 percent a year in the late 1970s, and increased by roughly 3 percent a year in the 1980s.

Direct financial aid played a relatively minor role in the financing of higher education prior to the creation and expansion of government student aid programs beginning in the 1960s. Before then, student aid was limited to scholarships provided by colleges and universities, private organizations (like the Kiwanis), and foundations. With the expansion in federal aid, however, private and philanthropic aid has diminished in importance.

The tuition benefits provided by employers are another source of nongovernment aid. This form of aid appears to have grown over time. Employees find this to be a valuable benefit, and since 1978 they have been allowed to exclude it from their taxable income. However, this tax provision has been the subject of considerable legislative wrangling. In several instances benefits have had to be enacted retroactively because the provision's sunset limitation had already occurred.

Federal aid to students expanded tremendously after the Second World War with the passage of the GI Bill, which provided aid in return for service and thus enabled millions of veterans of that conflict and of the Korean and Vietnam wars to pay for their college education. The National Defense Education Act of 1958 marked a change in this philosophy. Its emphasis was on fellowship and loan programs that sought to encourage students to continue their higher education, principally in the sciences and engineering.

Another dimension was added to the federal role in 1965 with the passage of the Higher Education Act, which increased educational opportunities for economically disadvantaged students. Historically, this group has been substantially underrepresented in America's colleges and universities. In response to pressures for tuition tax credits or deductions, the 1965 legislation also established the guaranteed student loan (GSL) program to provide moderately subsidized loans for students from middle-income families. Coincidentally, the social security legislation was also amended in 1965 to extend benefits to college-age dependents enrolled in postsecondary educational programs.

The federal equal opportunity theme was greatly reinforced in 1972 with the introduction of the basic educational opportunity grant program (renamed Pell grants in 1980 after the program's chief Senate sponsor), which provided a base level of financial support for any financially needy individual enrolled in postsecondary education. In 1978 the Middle Income Student Assistance Act increased the income eligibility levels for both the basic grant and GSL programs, as in 1965, as an alternative to proposed tax-credit legislation.

The 1980s witnessed more gradual increases in student aid combined with a small degree of retrenchment. Although the GSL program imposed some additional fees on borrowers and restrictions on eligibility, the volume of loans continued to grow. College benefits for the dependents of social security recipients were phased out completely, and GI Bill expenditures decreased as the number of eligible veterans dropped. At the same time, overall funding for Pell grants and the size of the average grant increased faster than inflation. However, most of this additional funding was absorbed by the increased numbers of low-income recipients in noncollegiate vocational programs. As a result, increases in the maximum Pell grant lagged behind the general rate of inflation and even further behind the increases in college tuitions.

The expansion in federal student aid coincided with the growth of state and institutional aid efforts, although the growth in the number of states that provide grant assistance was no coincidence: in 1972 the federal government launched the state student incentive grant program to encourage states to establish their own programs of grant assistance. Today all the states administer at least one grant program, and most states have authorized more than one grant effort. The states in 1988 collectively spent about $1.6 billion on these grant programs, which represents more than a 50 percent increase over spending in 1980 and a small increase in real terms. On a per recipient basis, however, state grants have declined in real terms since 1980, for the number of recipients has grown far faster than overall funding.

There are also three federal programs that allocate matching funds to colleges and universities for grants, work-study positions, and loans to needy students. Federal funding for these campus-based programs fell by nearly 20 percent in real terms in the 1980s, whereas the student aid support that institutions provide from their own funds increased rapidly, especially at private institutions.

In view of the growing use of internally funded aid in recent years, some analysts have questioned whether reported tuition increases overstate the change in price that students are actually paying. Indeed, the tuition and fees net of this aid, which are a more accurate measure of price, have not increased as fast as the sticker price over time. The trend in net prices helps to explain why enrollments have not fallen during a period of rapid tuition increases.

The next important question to consider is how the growth in student aid overall compares with the increase in college costs. Before World War II, the aid students received from governments, educational institutions, and private sources combined amounted to less than 10 percent of the total costs of attendance. The rest was paid by students or their parents. Since that time, with the evolution of federal student aid programs, the amount of student aid available from all sources has constituted a much larger share of the total costs of attendance.

Student aid from all sources peaked above 40 percent of total costs of attendance in both 1975 and 1980 (figure 1). The peak in 1975 was largely the result of the growth in GI Bill expenditures as Vietnam-era veterans used their benefits. In 1980 student aid once again increased, with the expansion in the basic (Pell) grant and GSL programs brought about by the 1978 middle-income student legislation. Between 1980 and 1982 student aid as a percentage of costs of attendance declined sharply, principally because of the 1981 budget reconciliation legislation and the phasing out of the social security educational benefits. Since 1982 aid as a proportion of costs has hovered around 30 percent.[5]

5. Estimates of the amount of student aid are drawn from College Board, *Trends in Student Aid* (Washington, various years). The total costs of attendance are calculated by multiplying average costs of attendance by full-time-equivalent enrollments, both drawn from U.S. Department of Education, *Digest of Education*

FIGURE 1. Student Aid as a Percentage of Total Costs
of Attendance, by Type of Aid, 1970–87

Percent of cost

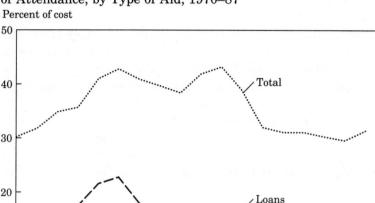

SOURCES: College Board, *Trends in Student Aid* (Washington, various years); and U.S. Department of Education, *Digest of Education Statistics,* various years.

The patterns in aid availability have varied for different types of aid, as figure 1 also shows. Grant aid increased from less than 10 percent of the total costs of attendance in 1970 to over 15 percent by the end of the decade. Since 1980 grant aid has fallen back to roughly 13 percent of the total costs of attendance. The availability of service-related aid—in the form of veterans' and social security educational benefits as well as college work-study programs—has dropped from 20 percent of the total costs of attendance in 1975 to about 2 percent in 1987.

Loans as a percentage of the total costs of attendance jumped from 7 percent in 1975 to more than 15 percent in the early 1980s. Many people have expressed concern about this trend in

Statistics. The costs of attending proprietary institutions were estimated from data submitted by those proprietary schools that apply for federal student aid.

borrowing because it could be having an adverse effect on students' educational, career, and personal decisions, and could produce more loan defaults.

Another means of measuring the relative adequacy of student aid is to compare the specific amounts of aid that students can receive with their costs of attendance. The maximum Pell grant and maximum GSL have declined substantially as a percentage of the average total costs of attendance in both public and private institutions (table 1). The Pell grant maximum in 1987 was less than two-fifths of the average total costs at public institutions (it was nearly two-thirds in 1975) and about one-fifth of the costs of attending private institutions (which is down from one-third in 1975).

The maximum GSL was larger than the average total costs of attending public institutions in 1975, but met only about half of those costs in 1987. At private institutions, a GSL covered more than half of the total costs of attendance in 1975, but less than one-quarter of the costs in 1987.

After more than a decade of no change, the 1986 reauthorization of the Higher Education Act raised the loan maximum for upper-division undergraduates as well as graduate and professional school students, but left the maximum loan essentially unchanged for freshmen and sophomores. It also renamed GSL as Stafford loans (after Robert Stafford, Republican senator from Vermont). Authorities are reluctant to increase loan limits in all categories because the GSL program is already expensive—every loan dollar costs the federal government 30 to 50 cents in interest and default expenditures, depending on the prevailing Treasury bill rate. Concern about the growing imbalance between grants and loans has also led the government to keep loan limits down.

A slightly different picture emerges when the average Pell grant and GSL are compared with the costs of attendance. Between 1980 and 1987 the average Pell grant increased by almost half, which is faster than the increase in the maximum award, but slower than the increase in college costs over the same period. In the Stafford loan program, most students borrow the maximum, and therefore the average loan has not changed much over time.

Shifts in Demographic and Participation Patterns

The growing need for alternative forms of financing also stems from the changing dynamics of college enrollments. In particular, there are fewer students of traditional college age and more older ones; the participation of minority and low-income students has failed to increase; and rising tuitions have caused many middle-income students to choose lower-priced institutions.

Changing Demographics

The number of people in the traditional college-age population of eighteen- to twenty-four-year-olds increased from 16 million in 1960 to 25 million in 1970 and peaked at 30 million in 1980. The number of public high school graduates grew from 1.6 million in 1960 to 2.6 million in 1970 and peaked at 2.8 million in the mid-1970s. The doubling in the size of the college-age group and the 75 percent increase in the number of high school graduates served both as the stimulus and the fuel for the rapid expansion in college enrollments in the 1960s and 1970s.[6]

Since 1980 these trends have reversed direction. The size of the traditional college-age group has been declining and is expected to bottom out in the mid-1990s at a level 20 percent or more below its peak at the start of the 1980s. In the mid-1980s the annual number of high school graduates had dropped 15 percent from its peak in the mid-1970s. Many colleges and universities see the dwindling applicant pool, combined with inadequate financing options, as a formula for disaster over the next decade.

The fact is, however, that college enrollments have not declined as predicted, principally because an increasing number of older students have enrolled. Participation rates among traditional college-age youth have also increased slightly. The growth in the

6. Population statistics are from U.S. Bureau of the Census, *Current Population Reports,* series P-25, various years. High school graduate figures are from U.S. Department of Education, Digest of Education Statistics (1988).

TABLE 1. Pell Grants and Stafford (GSL) Loans as a Proportion of College Costs of Attendance, 1970–87
Current dollars

Year	Maximum award	Average award	Maximum award as percent of average cost		Average award as percent of average cost	
			Public	Private	Public	Private
			PELL GRANTS			
1970	0	0	0.0	0.0	0.0	0.0
1971	0	0	0.0	0.0	0.0	0.0
1972	0	0	0.0	0.0	0.0	0.0
1973	452	270	22.5	12.4	13.4	7.4
1974	1,050	628	49.7	26.6	29.7	15.9
1975	1,400	761	61.8	32.8	33.6	17.8
1976	1,400	759	57.8	30.8	31.8	16.7
1977	1,400	758	54.8	29.0	29.6	15.7
1978	1,600	814	58.8	30.5	29.9	15.5
1979	1,800	929	60.5	31.5	31.2	16.2
1980	1,750	882	53.2	27.4	26.8	13.8
1981	1,670	849	45.8	23.2	23.1	11.8
1982	1,800	959	44.8	22.5	23.9	12.0
1983	1,800	1,014	42.2	20.9	23.8	11.8
1984	1,900	1,111	41.6	20.8	24.3	11.9
1985	2,100	1,279	43.4	20.9	26.4	12.7
1986	2,100	1,301	41.5	19.6	25.7	12.1
1987	2,100	1,350	39.7	18.2	25.5	11.7

		STAFFORD LOANS (GSL)			
1970	1,500	918	87.2	47.3	53.4	28.9
1971	1,500	992	82.9	44.5	54.8	29.4
1972	2,500	1,113	129.9	71.3	57.8	31.8
1973	2,500	1,196	124.2	68.3	59.4	32.7
1974	2,500	1,225	118.3	63.2	58.0	31.0
1975	2,500	1,312	110.3	58.6	57.9	30.8
1976	2,500	1,401	103.1	55.0	57.8	30.8
1977	2,500	1,593	97.5	51.7	62.1	33.0
1978	2,500	1,819	91.9	47.7	66.8	34.7
1979	2,500	1,982	84.0	43.7	66.6	34.6
1980	2,500	2,086	76.0	39.1	63.4	32.7
1981	2,500	2,206	67.9	34.7	59.9	30.6
1982	2,500	2,230	82.2	31.3	55.5	27.9
1983	2,500	2,266	58.6	29.0	53.1	26.3
1984	2,500	2,312	54.7	26.7	50.6	24.7
1985	2,500	2,307	51.7	24.8	47.7	22.9
1986	2,500	2,359	49.4	23.3	46.6	22.0
1987	2,625a	2,466	49.6	22.7	46.6	21.4

SOURCES: College Board, *Trends in Student Aid* (Washington, various years); and U.S. Department of Education, *Digest of Education Statistics*, various years.
a. For first- and second-year students. For upperclassmen the maximum loan is $4,000.

older, nontraditional student population cannot reasonably be attributed to any increase in the financial aid being made available to these students. By and large, the grant, work-study, and loan programs remain targeted on the traditional college-age student. The increase in older students appears to be more a function of enhanced recruiting by colleges and a greater awareness that additional education and training will make a difference in the lives of these individuals.

The new financing mechanisms discussed in this volume are directed primarily at the traditional college-age student. Most of the new savings, loans, assured access, and service proposals would not apply to older, nontraditional college students. Other financing mechanisms may be needed to address the needs of this rapidly expanding group.

Changing Participation Patterns

Although the rates at which Americans participate in higher education are the highest in the world and still seem to be rising slightly, the past decade has seen some troubling shifts in participation, especially among minority and low-income students. The number of minority students attending elementary and secondary school and graduating from high school has increased greatly since the mid-1960s. Minorities now account for slightly less than one-third of all public school students, and the percentage of minorities completing high school has increased. According to data from the *Current Population Survey* (CPS), the proportion of blacks aged eighteen to twenty-four who completed high school in 1986 or received a general equivalency diploma was over 75 percent, compared with an 83 percent completion rate for white students. The high school completion rate for Hispanics in 1986 was 60 percent.[7]

Despite these increases, the percentage of minority students participating in higher education appears to be falling. In 1975, after a decade of progress, the percentage of black high school

7. Bureau of the Census, *Current Population Survey,* series p-20, various years.

graduates aged eighteen to twenty-four who were enrolled in or had completed at least one year of college was 48 percent, but by 1985 that percentage had fallen to 44 percent. For Hispanics, the participation rate fell from 49 to 47 percent. In contrast, the proportion of white high school graduates enrolling in college rose slightly, from 52 percent in 1975 to 55 percent in 1985. There is some controversy over these figures and their interpretation. For example, an increasing proportion of black high school graduates apparently now go into the military or enroll in proprietary school vocational programs and therefore do not appear in the college enrollment statistics. Even so, the participation in college by minority groups continues to decline and remains a cause for concern.

A principal goal of the federal student aid legislation is to increase the participation of economically disadvantaged students in postsecondary education. But the available data suggest that little progress has been made toward the achievement of this goal over the past decade. The CPS statistics indicate that the proportion of college students from low-income families did increase during the 1970s, but that from 1975 to 1985 it fell, from over 40 percent to about 33 percent. Moreover, according to a longitudinal study of 1980 high school graduates, students with low socioeconomic status who are in the highest achievement quartile are one-third less likely to go to college than equally able students from families with the highest socioeconomic status.[8] To the extent that student aid programs should be most effective in helping to narrow the difference in participation among the brightest students, this lack of progress is disheartening.

Nonetheless, much of the public outcry about the difficulty of paying for college and most of the innovative financing mechanisms that have been developed in recent years have tended to focus on students from middle-class families. The argument is that rapid increases in college charges, combined with restricted

8. Information on the participation of lowest-income students is from Bureau of the Census, "Current Population Reports," unpublished tabulations; and U.S. Department of Education, National Center for Education Statistics, *High School and Beyond* (1988).

eligibility for student aid, have created a squeeze on the middle class. To alleviate this squeeze, it is necessary to make adequate financing available, although it need not be on a highly subsidized basis.

The eligibility of middle-income students for student aid has varied over time. Initially, students from middle-income families were ineligible for Pell grants since the program was set up to help the most needy students. Eligibility for Pell grants was expanded under the Middle Income Student Assistance Act of 1978, but was again restricted beginning in 1982–83. Thus students with a family income at the intermediate level (as defined by the Bureau of Labor Statistics) became eligible for roughly $500 in Pell grants in the 1979–80 academic year, but the average award for these students fell to about $300 in 1981–82, and by 1982–83, they were again ineligible.[9] The 1986 amendments to the Higher Education Act loosened eligibility standards for many of these students through changes in the way that family contributions are calculated, although funding levels have precluded most of these students from actually receiving awards.

When the GSL program was created in 1965, only students from families earning less than $15,000 a year were eligible for subsidized loans. Students from higher-income families could borrow, but without government subsidy; roughly 5 percent of all GSLs were made to these students. In 1976 this income standard was raised to $25,000. In 1978 the income cap was lifted altogether, and all students, regardless of their family income, could borrow at subsidized rates.

The budget reconciliation legislation of 1981 restored an income cap in GSL, but it differed from the pre-1978 version. Students below $30,000 of adjusted family income (with income defined differently from before 1978) could continue to obtain loans on which the federal government paid the interest while they were in school. Students with family incomes above $30,000 could also obtain these subsidized loans if they could demonstrate financial

9. Thomas Mortenson, *Pell Grant Program Changes and Their Effects on Applicant Eligibility, 1973–74 to 1988–89* (Iowa City: American College Testing Program, May 1988).

need, with need defined as the costs of attendance in excess of other resources, including the family's contribution. In 1986 the rules were again changed so that now all students have to demonstrate financial need in order to qualify for a subsidized GSL.

These legislative changes of the 1980s have restricted the eligibility of middle-income students for federal student aid subsidies through grants and loans. However, they do not appear to have forced many middle-income students to forgo their plans for a higher education. Instead, they seem to have contributed to increased enrollments of middle-class students at lower-priced public institutions. Evidence of this is an annual survey of college freshmen which indicates that the median family income of students enrolling in public four-year colleges and universities has increased relative to the family incomes of freshmen enrolling in private four-year colleges.[10]

These recent restrictions on the eligibility of middle-income students have perhaps played a more critical role in the development of innovative financing mechanisms than any of the other factors discussed in this chapter. The politically vocal middle class, seeing its eligibility for traditional student aid programs slipping, called on politicians for help. Whereas the help it received in 1978 was an expansion in the existing federal student aid programs, the trend in the 1980s has been toward new financing plans, tuition guarantees, and tax incentives to encourage saving for college. The evolution of these savings and tuition guarantee plans is discussed in the next chapter.

10. Higher Education Research Institute, *The American Freshmen: Twenty Year Trends* (Los Angeles, 1987).

Chapter Two

Tuition Prepayments, Guarantees, and Savings Plans

Tuition prepayments, guarantees, and savings plans are all based on the idea that early savings or payments for college are advantageous because they allow parents to avoid or alleviate the effects of rising college charges. This idea has recently become one of the most hotly debated topics among those concerned with finding new mechanisms for financing higher education. Although the incentives to save and prepay tuition have taken a variety of forms, debates on these plans turn in large measure on two questions. What benefits are available to parents and others who participate in these plans? And who pays for these benefits?

Tuition Prepayments

The wave of interest in tuition guarantees in the 1980s began as a ripple in the late 1970s when tuition prepayment plans were introduced at a handful of institutions, including Washington University in St. Louis and the University of Southern California. These prepayment plans provided a means of "frontloading" four years of tuition once the student was accepted for admission. By paying all four years of tuition at the time of matriculation, a family can avoid paying for tuition increases during the time the student is earning a degree. The growing number of families who choose this type of financing would seem to confirm the public opinion polls that suggest many parents believe college tuition will continue to rise faster than inflation and the after-tax rate of return on their investments.

The college or university, for its part, is able to use these funds in advance of incurring the actual costs of educating the student. The number of institutions that now offer these kinds of prepayment plans as part of their package of financing options has increased markedly, especially in the private sector. Most higher-priced private colleges and universities now offer at least some financing options along these lines. One possible concern about the growing popularity of this form of prepayment is that its extensive use by some parents could tend to push up the rate of tuition increases in the future for those students whose families do not prepay. Since it was first proposed, the prepayment concept has evolved in at least two directions: prepayment combined with loans, and tuition guarantees.

Prepayment Combined with Loans

The prepayment option can be tied in with a loan that allows families to borrow enough for the sizable outlay required to prepay four years' worth of tuition, which at today's prices can equal or exceed $50,000. The University of Pennsylvania is perhaps the best example of an institution that has aggressively combined tuition prepayment with loans. Its Penn plan, which is among the most sophisticated of these prepayment plans, offers multiple options and a substantial lending operation through which parents can borrow nearly all the funds they need to cover four years of tuition prepayment.

The decision to borrow in order to prepay four years of tuition depends on whether parents believe that the after-tax cost of borrowing—which will be higher now that consumer interest payments are nondeductible—will be lower than the anticipated increase in tuition at the participating institution. Otherwise, the parents would be better off by not borrowing to make the tuition prepayment. It will be interesting to monitor the Penn plan's borrowing option to see whether usage declines as the deductibility of consumer interest payments is phased out of the tax code and as the after-tax return on savings increases because of reductions in marginal tax rates. One means of offsetting the anticipated decline in usage would be to transform this type of borrowing into a home equity loan, which would then still qualify for the interest deduction.

Tuition Guarantees

More recently prepayment has entailed advancing payments many years ahead of when the child is ready to enroll in college. This form of tuition prepayment allows parents to invest when the child is young, and with that investment to pay all or a portion of tuition when the child is ready to enroll in college. These plans have been popularly dubbed tuition guarantees because the payments parents make today will fully cover the costs of tuition in the future when the child is ready to enroll, regardless of the list price of tuition at that time.

These plans have also been compared with commodities futures. In the futures market investors guess the future path of prices for any of a wide range of commodities and then buy either short or long, depending on their instincts. Unlike the commodities market, however, the tuition guarantee plans that currently exist do not have a system of puts and calls, nor does a liquid market exist for the buying and selling of tuitions futures. Several private concerns are in the process of developing tuition prepayment plans that would be negotiable and transferable among parties and therefore would be more like actual futures.

Tuition guarantees were first introduced at the institutional level. In 1985 Duquesne University in Pittsburgh announced that it would offer its alumni and others the opportunity to invest funds when their children were young and that the investment would cover fully the price of tuition when the child was ready to enroll at Duquesne. But this investment opportunity was not a guarantee of admission. If the student was not admitted to, or did not choose to attend Duquesne, the parents would be refunded their initial investment, but with little or no interest. The initial contract was priced at a considerable discount from Duquesne's tuition at the time. Officials adopted this discounting strategy because they thought the institution might have trouble filling its seats in the future, but they also believed that if the fund's investment proceeds were sufficient to cover the school's marginal cost, the plan would be economically viable.

Duquesne received a good deal of publicity when it introduced its plan, and at least a dozen other institutions decided to sign up with the firm that had helped develop the idea. Less than three years later, Duquesne suspended the plan, explaining that a drop in anticipated investment return, occasioned in part by the October 1987 stock market collapse and new projections of future tuition increases, made it infeasible to continue offering the tuition guarantee option. What is curious about Duquesne's decision is why it did not raise the price of the contract for new participants above the projected marginal cost (but still keep it below the anticipated average cost), rather than abandon the plan entirely.

Even before Duquesne announced it was going to suspend the plan, interest had declined because the plan restricted the parents' investment opportunities and did not offer the student a choice of institution. The adverse publicity generated by the decision to suspend operations will most likely extinguish whatever interest the idea may have generated at other institutions.

When it was first formulated, the Duquesne idea attracted the attention of James Blanchard, the governor of Michigan, and Robert Bowman, the state's treasurer, who saw in it the potential for applying a tuition guarantee at the state level. In their view, the trouble with Duquesne's plan was that it provided no choice of institution. They reasoned that if the guarantee of tuition was applied to a wider range of institutions—for example, to all public colleges and universities within a state—it would appeal to a broader range of families. They proceeded to formulate an alternative plan, which the state legislature passed and signed into law in December 1986.

Under the Michigan plan, families make payments into a state-managed investment fund. Families investing in the fund are assured that their payments will cover the full tuition at any public institution in the state when the child is ready for college. Like the Duquesne plan, however, participation in the Michigan plan does not represent a guarantee of admission. Students must first be admitted to a public institution within the state. Students

attending a private or an out-of-state institution are eligible to
receive an amount equal to the value of what they would have
received if they had attended a Michigan public institution.
Refunds for unused funds would be set at the amount of the
initial investment, either with no accrual of interest or with
earnings, depending on which type of several plans had been
purchased.

It should be emphasized that the Michigan plan does not
attempt to guarantee that the amount of the parents' investment
plus interest will equal tuition at the time the child is ready to
enroll. Instead, it assures parents that their payments will serve
in lieu of tuition regardless of whether the amount they invested
plus interest is sufficient to pay tuition costs when the child is
ready to enroll. The central issue surrounding the Michigan and
similar guarantee plans is who makes up the difference when
the principal plus investment return is less than the stated
tuition.

To encourage participation in the plan, the Michigan legislation
allows parents to deduct investments in the fund from their state
taxable income and has exempted fund buildup from state income
tax. (No provision is made for the recapture of tax benefits if
funds are not used to pay for college expenses.) Of greater interest
to the bill's sponsors was how the Internal Revenue Service would
view this arrangement. If the investment income is allowed to
accumulate free of federal income tax, then the plan becomes
much more attractive. Plan proponents argued that the investment should be viewed as a prepaid contract for services, and
that the fund's inside buildup should therefore be exempt from
federal income taxation. Others countered that if students are
given a choice of institutions, the plan differs little in its effect
from a private mutual fund, and should therefore be taxed. This
taxation issue was considered important enough to delay imple-
menting the plan until the legislation obtained a favorable IRS
ruling.

After more than a year of negotiation and waiting, the IRS
responded to the state's request for a private letter ruling on this
taxability issue. The IRS indicated that the fund buildup in the
Michigan trust will be considered income spread over four years

of college attendance and will be taxed at the child's rate of taxation. In addition, the IRS indicated that the trust itself might be taxed for a portion of the fund buildup.

The sponsors of the Michigan plan declared that the IRS ruling was favorable and proceeded to make plans for implementation. A more reasoned opinion might be that there were three possible ways the IRS could have ruled: it could have taxed the fund buildup at the parent's tax rate, at the child's rate, or not at all. The IRS chose the middle route, which, in combination with the possibility that the fund may be taxed as well, will make the Michigan plan a less attractive investment opportunity to families.

The response to the Michigan plan has been instructive. In August 1988, when the plan began to sell contracts, there was an outpouring of interest: more than 80,000 families made a nominal deposit that would enable them to participate in the plan. The number exceeded even the expectations of the plan's sponsors. By November 1988 some 27,000 families had actually signed up, investing nearly $200 million.

Many of these families apparently financed their investment by borrowing, mostly through banks and savings and loans in the state. The use of loans to finance tuition guarantees opens up further questions about the advisability of the plan. To be in the parents' (if not the student's) best interest, the return on the investment in the guarantee fund must exceed the after-tax interest rate that parents pay on the loans they borrow. To the extent that the interest on these loans will no longer be eligible for tax deductions, the tuition guarantee plan will be that much less of a good deal for those parents who borrow in order to participate in it.

The publicity and enthusiasm surrounding the announcement of the Michigan plan and its subsequent enactment stimulated tremendous interest in other states, all of which requested information on the plan. Many states studied and debated the merits of the Michigan approach, and by the end of 1989 a dozen states had passed bills similar or identical to the Michigan legislation. In three states (Michigan, Florida, and Wyoming) the guarantee plans had become operational by 1989. In each of the other states, implementation of the enabling legislation was delayed until the IRS issued a ruling, since one characteristic of a private letter ruling is that it does not apply to any other case, no matter how similar it might be.

Even without a favorable tax ruling, the Michigan and other guarantee plans may still turn out to be a good deal for participating families. Such a guarantee is still of value to parents who worry about their ability to pay the future level of tuitions, particularly if the futures contract is underpriced relative to current tuitions, as was the case in Michigan. Most of the states that looked into the Michigan plan, however, decided against adopting it, mainly because of the sizable contingent financial liability involved.

Tuition guarantees of this nature are somewhat analogous to a defined benefit pension plan, in that the future payment of tuition is made irrespective of how well the fund performs. Past experience with defined benefit pension plans may be helpful in explaining the risks attached to tuition guarantees. Over the life of a defined benefit plan, one of two things may happen: either the plan will accumulate assets in excess of the benefits it will have to pay out, or the assets will be insufficient to cover the projected benefit levels. If the plan's assets exceed benefit needs, the employer has the option under current law to reclaim the "surplus." This is what has happened in a number of instances, including some well-publicized leveraged buyout situations; the company in these cases pays out the projected benefits and gets to keep the remaining surplus. This would be comparable to a tuition guarantee plan in which tuition increases lagged behind investment returns. In such a case, the state presumably could recapture the surplus and use it to pay for other benefits.

Of greater concern would be a case in which tuitions increase faster than the annual rate of return on the investment. This would be similar to a defined benefit plan that did not accumulate enough assets to pay out full benefits and was thus left with an unfunded liability. Either the employer would have to replenish the fund to cover these liabilities, or the retired employees would have to accept lower benefit levels than they were promised. Given the enormous unfunded liabilities that defined benefit pension plans have generated in both the public and the private sectors, legislators in most of the states have apparently been reluctant to create a new contingent liability in the form of a tuition guarantee plan that works on a principle similar to that of defined benefit pension plans.

Tuition guarantee plans, however, need not involve a state financial commitment or a contingent liability. If the state does not make itself liable, then somebody else can assume the risk and pay the benefit provided for families whose investment rises more slowly than tuition increases. In part, the difference can be made up by other families in the plan whose investment rises more quickly than tuitions. In this sense, the Michigan plan can be viewed as an insurance plan. Families whose investment goes up more slowly than tuitions increase would be insured by those families who joined at a time when the return to the fund was greater than the increase in tuitions. This second set of families will realize in retrospect that they would have been better off investing their funds elsewhere, but to the extent they participated knowingly, they essentially paid an insurance premium on which they did not collect.

As long as a tuition guarantee plan is financed entirely by its participants, issues of public policy are not all that relevant. They become important if it turns out that the plan is not self-financing, a situation that could occur under several conditions. Michigan, as in the case of the suspended Duquesne plan, offered shares in the fund at a substantial discount from current tuition prices. For a newborn child, the payment in 1988 was $1,689, which was about one-third less than the tuition for the University of Michigan at that time. Although such a discount is certainly one way to keep people interested in the idea, it also puts self-financing on a shaky basis.

Moreover, if tuitions should increase faster than the fund's investment return, discounting is akin to providing a grant for families who participate in the plan. Not only would the state be providing insurance against tuition inflation, but it would also be providing a sizable premium deduction. The public policy concern is that the state may end up subsidizing middle- and upper-income families in the plan at an amount that is as large as or larger than what the state provides for students from impoverished family circumstances. (In 1987–88 the maximum grant Michigan offered students at public institutions was $1,200.)

It is also possible that the educational institution will end up paying for the benefit. It may simply accept what it receives from the fund, even though the payment is less than what the institution is charging when the child enrolls. If the institution were to forgo the difference between the fund's payout and its stated tuition, then the policy would not have a negative effect on consumers. The policy could add to the precariousness of the institution's financial position, however, if it would otherwise have been possible to substitute a higher or full payer for the plan participant.

What is more likely is that nonparticipants in the plan will end up paying in the form of higher tuitions. A state or an institution in which the guarantee fund has appreciated at a slower rate than tuition will be sorely tempted to raise the tuitions charged to those students who have not participated in the plan in order to make up for lost revenues. Thus parents and students who were either unable or unwilling to save early and participate in the guarantee plan would have to pay for the benefits provided for families in the form of a tuition guarantee. This would be a highly undesirable policy outcome of a tuition guarantee plan.

Alternatively, if institutions cannot raise their prices because of competitive pressures or because state legislators will not allow it, they may be forced to reduce the quality of the education they provide in order to stay within their budgets. None of these plans, after all, can claim to guarantee the quality of the education that will be provided.

Regardless of how the benefit is paid for and who pays it, tuition guarantees remain essentially a means of relieving relatively wealthy families of the worry of constantly increasing tuitions. If the precaution was unnecessary—that is, if tuitions were to increase more slowly than investment returns—then participants would have bought insurance they did not need. But if the insurance policy "pays off," then someone has to pay for providing them with this peace of mind, whether it be the state taxpayers, other plan participants, or other students. The possibility that such a subsidy might occur and that others might have to pay for it is what makes the guarantee concept questionable public policy.

Another concern about the Michigan plan is that the guarantee will apply only to public institutions, where the payment of tuition is not nearly the obstacle it is in the private sector. Under the Michigan plan, the students who are helped most attend institutions that are already heavily subsidized by the state. Considerably less assistance is provided through guarantees and other state support to students who attend less subsidized private institutions, where tuitions average several times more than in the public sector. Therefore, it is not surprising to discover that private institutions are typically not enthusiastic about guarantee plans modeled after the Michigan approach.

The development of state tuition guarantee plans has also stimulated considerable private sector interest. Several private organizations have now initiated tuition guarantee plans of their own in which the guarantee benefit may be used at participating educational institutions. The critical issue in these private tuition guarantee plans will be how many colleges are willing to participate. Typically, the plans entice schools either by providing upfront payments or by turning over to the institutions most of the investment capital. Without such enticements, it makes little sense for institutions to participate, since they are in effect agreeing to accept less than what they otherwise would charge for tuition. But institutional officials should consider what obligations they are assuming by participating in these private plans, particularly the fact that the institution may be losing considerable revenues in the future. Even with enticements, it does not seem likely that many institutions will opt to participate in these private guarantee plans.

State Savings Plans

After studying the Michigan plan, most states have decided to encourage savings without providing a guarantee against future tuition increases. Such a plan is analogous to a defined contribution pension plan, wherein each person's investment rests on its own foundation. What your investment earns is what you receive. Unlike a defined benefit plan such as Michigan's, where a contingent liability may exist, a defined contribution college savings plan does not create a future obligation beyond the scope of the investment return.

For many years New York was the only state with a college savings plan. Its parents and student savings (PASS) program allowed state residents to deduct up to $750 every year from their state taxable income for funds that they paid into a college savings account. Even though the state's income tax rates are relatively high, PASS was used by a very small proportion of parents, less than 5 percent of state taxpayers. Ironically, the PASS provision was phased out in 1987 just as enthusiasm for college savings plans was growing.

Missouri was one of the first states in recent years to break from the Michigan approach and venture instead into a savings plan without a guarantee. It passed a plan similar to New York's PASS plan in which deductions are provided for contributions to college savings accounts and the interest on the savings is exempt from state taxation.

Illinois was the first state to adopt a state-based college savings plan that used federally tax-exempt bonds as the savings instrument. Under legislation enacted in November 1987, Illinois families may buy a zero-coupon general obligation bond that the state uses to finance many of its capital needs. If a family then holds the bond for at least five years and the proceeds are used to pay for college-related expenses, the state agrees to make a supplemental interest payment that may be as much as four-tenths of a percentage point a year above the interest that the state would normally pay on that bond. This supplemental payment, which the state would pay out of general funds, is intended to encourage parents to save more for their children's education.

Although the value of these bonds is only marginally better than the rate of return on other tax-exempt bonds, the initial $90 million offering was gobbled up in a matter of days from the handful of banks that were selling them. One of the Chicago papers ran a front-page headline proclaiming "Bond Mania." A second offering in September 1988 of $225 million was also quickly subscribed. The success of these initial offerings was probably not so much a function of marketing and publicity—small advertisements were run in a dozen newspapers around the state announcing the bond sale—as it was a reflection of the growing concern among many families about the future path of tuitions. It may also be that many of the buyers of these specially designated bonds would have bought other, less attractive tax-exempt bonds if these had not been available.

The Illinois plan appears to have replaced the Michigan plan as the model that other states are considering as a means of encouraging greater savings for college. Nearly two dozen states had passed some form of savings legislation by the end of 1989, and a number of other states still actively looking into the issue appear to be inclined to use tax-exempt bonds as a vehicle for college savings. Most of these other states seem persuaded by the simplicity of the Illinois approach, its use of an already existing and reliable financial instrument that provides federal tax benefits, and its decision not to burden the state with an unknowable and unpredictable contingent liability, such as the kind of tuition guarantees may carry.[1]

One question raised by savings incentives like the Illinois plan is whether they do produce additional savings, or simply convince a set of parents to switch their savings from one instrument to another with little or no increase in the overall savings rate. Most of these bonds have probably been bought by investors who planned to buy tax-exempt bonds anyway, and saw this as a way to raise their return slightly. From a policy perspective, it is difficult to limit the benefit to those families who change their behavior. Instead, the benefit will typically be provided for all investors whose children attend participating institutions, including those parents who would have saved anyway.

A related question is whether it is desirable to add to the rate

1. Much of the information on what the states are doing in college savings and tuition guarantee plans has been obtained from the Education Commission of the States (ECS). See, for example, "1989 Survey of College Savings and Guaranteed Tuition Programs," ECS, Denver, Colorado, September 1989.

of return for families who use the bonds to pay for college expenses. On the one hand, some incentive is needed to prod families to save more than they already do to meet the cost of college; without an additional rate of return, there appears to be little reason for families to save more for their children's college expenses. Rewarding prudent parents and raising the overall savings rate are certainly worthwhile policy goals. On the other hand, since the families who buy these bonds are predominantly in the higher-income brackets, the benefits derived from this extra return will go mostly to upper-income groups, a development that may not be regarded as equitable.

One way to address this equity concern would be to offer the additional rate of return only to families from more moderate circumstances. For example, an income test could be applied to limit the distribution of the subsidy. Or, more simply, the extra return might only be provided to students who qualified for state grant assistance. Any provision to target benefits to less well-to-do parents, however, will most likely reduce participation and may well seem too complex.

Federal Savings Incentives

The same concerns that have led to the development of tuition guarantee and savings plans in the states have generated interest at the federal level in encouraging families to save more for their children's college education. To many observers, a federal savings plan seems superior to the plans offered by individual states; it would give participants a greater choice of institutions in that benefits would not be limited to particular state institutions. This encouragement of student mobility across state lines is seen as a distinct advantage of a federal or national savings plan. In addition, to the extent that inadequate savings for college is seen as a national problem, many feel it requires a national solution.

Often lost in the recent discussions about the need for greater federal incentives to save for college is the fact that the federal tax code for many years contained a number of provisions that encouraged parents to save for their children. These provisions ranged from the fairly straightforward to the truly arcane. The simplest was the provision that allowed parents and others to make gifts to minors (up to $10,000 per year per giver) in which the income from those gifts would be taxed at the child's tax rate. The more complicated provisions included a set of trust and loan arrangements that usually required the expertise of a tax lawyer or an estate planner and were used predominantly by wealthy people to escape taxation on their investments.

Perceived abuses in the use of these provisions led Congress to eliminate most of them in the 1986 tax reform legislation. But in doing so, Congress may have thrown out at least one baby with the bathwater. The 1986 legislation limits the amount of gifts on which income can be taxed at the child's rate when the child is younger than fourteen. This change was wrongheaded for at least two reasons. First, the Uniform Gift to Minors Act, when compared with other transfer mechanisms, is a provision that is used by moderate- and middle-income families as well as the wealthy. It has traditionally not been the provision of choice for wealthy parents who are trying to avoid taxation.

Moreover, the 1986 revisions impose a higher tax rate on the income from gifts precisely when, as a matter of policy, it would seem wise to encourage parents to save for college—when the child is young so that a substantial asset accumulation can occur. If the principal objective was to limit the use of gifts by higher-income families, a preferable approach would have been to reduce the amount of annual or cumulative gifts that could be made— say, reduce the annual limit from $10,000 to $5,000—rather than make a distinction on the basis of the child's age. Moreover, if an age distinction was going to be made, it should have been in the opposite direction: tax the income on gifts to children *over* the age of fourteen at their parents' rate.

The 1986 tax legislation left one provision standing that allowed tax-sheltered savings that can be used to pay for college: single-premium life insurance (SPLI). Under the SPLI concept, the single premium fully pays for a life insurance policy, and the cash value on that policy is allowed to accumulate tax free. Loans can then be taken against that cash value at little or no interest to be used for expenses such as the children's college education. Insurance companies and brokers aggressively advertised the availability and desirability of buying a single-premium policy, and this level of attention and publicity led Congress to narrow this loophole in a technical amendment to the tax code in 1988.

It is ironic that the push for a new federal tax incentive for college savings followed so closely on the heels of legislation that eliminated many of the incentives that previously existed. Proposals for new federal tax incentives for college savings fall into several categories. One calls for the creation of educational savings accounts similar to individual retirement accounts (IRAs) that became so popular in the 1970s and early 1980s, and the use of which Congress limited in the 1986 tax legislation. A related proposal would allow parents to withdraw without penalty the funds accumulated in their IRAs to pay for the college expenses of their children. Another would create a federally sponsored mutual fund that would invest the contributions of participants. Still another would not tax the buildup on U.S. savings bonds if it is used to pay for college expenses.

To encourage college savings, the federal government could also provide tax benefits for some or all of the state or private plans that are related to college savings. For example, Congress could reverse or alter the IRS ruling on the Michigan plan through superseding legislation. Or tax exemptions could be granted to categories of college savings plans that meet specified criteria. The tax-exempt bonds used in Illinois and other states are, in effect, taking advantage of existing federal tax exemptions for college savings.

In the last days of the 100th Congress in 1988, a college savings provision was added to the package of technical amendments to the 1986 tax reform legislation. The provision, whose chief sponsor was Senator Edward Kennedy of Massachusetts, exempts from taxation the interest on U.S. savings bonds if the proceeds are turned over to a college or university for the payment of tuition and fees. The exemption will apply for bonds purchased beginning in 1990. To prevent wealthy people from benefiting from this provision, the full exemption is limited to single taxpayers with incomes of less than $40,000 and joint filers with incomes under $60,000. The tax exemption is reduced for those with incomes above these limits, and no exemption is provided for those whose income exceeds $60,000 as single filers or $90,000 as joint filers. These income limits are to be adjusted annually to reflect inflation. To minimize the costs of an additional tax-expenditure item, parents can no longer claim an exemption for their children who are at least twenty-four years old and in college.

Advocates of the savings bond provision argue that it is a simple measure, relies on an existing and reliable financial instrument, and carries a relatively low price tag. The educational savings account approach would cost substantially more, since contributions would be tax deductible and income on the investment would typically be tax deferred. The idea of using IRAs for education has lost some of its luster as education lobbyists have come to realize that they will have to get in line with other interest groups, such as those representing housing and health care, in trying to pry open the use of IRA accounts for nonretirement purposes. Also, many economists believe that IRAs did not generate much new savings even when fully tax free or tax deferred; special-purpose IRAs are likely to generate even less. It would seem more appropriate for the private sector rather than the federal government to develop a college investment fund. And the granting of federal tax-exempt status to generic or specific nonfederal college savings and tuition guarantee plans tends to remove the federal government from the policymaking process.

The new savings bond provision, like other new federal incentives for college savings, however, may detract from tax reform, may divert resources from student aid efforts, and may not be as effective or as equitable as expected. Tax reformers argue that it is counterproductive to reopen the tax code for college savings after so many loopholes were closed in the 1986 legislation. Those who advocate a college savings provision also come up against advocates (including themselves) who lobby for other tax legislation related to higher education, such as employer-paid education assistance, tax exemption for fellowships and scholarships, and the deductibility of student loan interest.

Some lobbyists worry that a college savings provision in the tax code will detract from increased funding for other higher education programs, especially student aid. Some economists worry that a tax incentive for saving may be both inequitable (because the rich are the ones most likely to save and therefore to benefit) and ineffective (because it is likely to reward those persons who would have saved anyway). The issue is whether the after-tax rate of return will generate additional savings, or will simply help those families who were planning to save anyway. If the latter is true, then no additional subsidy would be justified.

The tax reform issue could be eliminated if the tax exemption were changed into a spending provision. For example, savings bonds could be made more attractive if they paid a higher return (and it was taxed) when the proceeds were used for college. This would also enhance the equity of the provision, since a higher return on the bonds would help moderate-income families more than an equivalent tax benefit, which would help those in the highest tax bracket the most.

Those who worry about the adverse effect of savings incentives on funding for student aid programs are faced with a paradox: they would be less worried if the cost (and the effectiveness) of the savings approach was relatively small. This still leaves open the question whether the provision will generate more savings than it costs in tax expenditures. Also, providing the tax exclusion for savings bonds places other college savings instruments at a disadvantage. Not surprisingly, advocates of other college savings approaches are now lobbying for an extension of the savings bond tax exemption to other financial instruments in order to provide a level playing field.

The savings bond provision in the form in which it was enacted also raises some other thorny administrative questions. For example, whose income is being measured to determine whether the income is excludable? If your Uncle Lou made the initial contribution, is it his income that is taken into consideration, or the family income of the student? And when is the income measured—at the time of contribution or when the student matriculates? Insofar as family incomes change over time, the donors may have made the contribution because they were eligible for the tax exclusion at that time, only to discover that they are no longer eligible when the student enrolls in college. The income limits were imposed to add to the equity of the plan, but these limits and their application sharply detract from the provision's overall simplicity and ease of administration.

Plans That Combine Savings and Guarantees

Organizations that are interested in developing incentives for college savings are typically faced with the decision of whether to go with a straight savings approach or to provide a guarantee against future tuition increases. But in some instances there has been an attempt to combine a savings plan with some form of a guarantee. Two such hybrid plans are discussed here.

The CollegeSure CD

A number of private plans to encourage savings for college already exist, and a great many more are being developed. Banks, mutual funds, and other financial institutions, recognizing the growing concerns of parents, are starting college savings plans as part of their portfolio of offerings and use these college plans prominently in their marketing.

The most well known and heavily advertised private sector plan for college savings thus far has been the CollegeSure CD, which was first offered in 1987. This instrument was developed by the College Savings Bank of Princeton, New Jersey, an FDIC-insured institution currently offering a single product. (The bank aggressively sought FDIC insurance to assure investors of the safety of their investment.)

The CollegeSure CD, as its name suggests, is a certificate of deposit where the rate of return is indexed to changes over time in college tuitions. Rather than being linked to a certain amount of future tuition, the CollegeSure CD offers a rate of return guaranteed to keep up with changes in college prices. Whatever the increase in college tuitions while the certificate is held, as measured by an index of college tuitions, the investor earns that return on the face value of the certificate.

To receive this indexed rate of return, however, parents and other investors must pay a premium or a fee based on the number of years until the child is ready to enroll in college. The bank charges this premium, which is likely to be 1 to 2 percent a year of the face amount times the number of years before enrollment, so that it can safely ensure that the rate of return on the certificate will be indexed to changes in college costs. But the payment of the premium in effect reduces the rate of return on the investment. Let's say that a parent invests $10,000 in the certificate and that the index of tuitions increases at 7 percent a year. If the parent pays a premium of 1 to 2 percent a year to purchase such a certificate, then the effective rate of return is 5 to 6 percent, and not the 7 percent that tuitions increased.

Moreover, although the bank advertises that the rate of return will be enough to keep up with tuition inflation, the return is in pre-tax dollars. Therefore, the after-tax rate of return will be less than the average increase in tuitions. With a marginal tax rate of 28 percent, the after-tax rate of return in the previous example would be about 4 percent, which is well below the 7 percent annual increase in tuitions. In view of the premium that has to be paid and the taxability of the return, one might well ask whether the parent would be better off investing in some other instrument.

The continued rapid growth in tuitions and the media attention paid to this fact ensures that additional private sector savings and guarantee plans will be developed. It will be interesting to monitor these activities to determine whether the private sector perceives that more profitable opportunities are available through tuition guarantees or through savings plans without guarantees.

The Massachusetts Plan

Governor Michael Dukakis of Massachusetts, in the wake of the interest in the Michigan guarantee and other savings approaches, and as part of his presidential campaign, developed a plan that combined elements of a savings plan, a tuition guarantee, and an indexed rate of return. Under the proposal, parents could invest in small-denomination tax-exempt bonds issued by the commonwealth. The rate of return on the bonds would be indexed to tuition changes over time, although what index would be used is not resolved. As with the CollegeSure CD, it is expected that parents would pay a premium on the bonds in order to receive this indexed rate of return. In addition, the state might pay part of the premium or agree to pay a higher interest rate than it normally would for tax-exempt bonds. Educational institutions that participated in the plan would have their names listed on the bonds; by doing so, they would agree to accept the bond principal plus the indexed rate of return in exchange for that part of the tuition represented by the initial investment. If, for example, an institution was charging $10,000 in tuition when an investment of $1,000 was made, the educational institution would agree to accept the bond proceeds in exchange for 10 percent of tuition if and when the child enrolled in that institution.

By combining features of guarantee and savings plans, the Massachusetts approach could benefit from the advantages of each. As in a straight savings approach, participants could invest less than the full amount of tuition and still receive a benefit, the savings could be used for more than just tuition, and the bonds could be used at any institution (although the guarantee feature applies only to participating institutions within the state). Since tax-exempt bonds would be used, the interest on the bonds would not be subject to federal income taxation. The rate of return on the bonds would be linked to increases in college tuitions. Participants in the plan could also benefit from the guarantee feature, since institutions that agreed to accept payments in lieu of tuition would be obligated to accept the payment from the fund regardless of what they charged for tuition when the child enrolled.

The Massachusetts plan, as well as some other guarantee plans, has also been advocated as a way of creating a receptive environment for cost containment, because the return on the bonds would be linked to average tuition increases. The theory is that institutions at which tuitions have increased more quickly than the average would receive less than their full tuition and therefore would be more likely to keep their price increases down. But the opposite result is more likely to occur. At institutions that agreed to accept bond payments in lieu of tuition, there would be an upward pressure on the tuitions charged to nonparticipants if investment income fell short of tuition increases and if participation in the plan was widespread. If an institution receives less from plan participants than it otherwise would receive in tuition, then it may well be forced to charge more to students who are not in the guarantee plan to make up for the shortfall in revenues.

The Massachusetts plan, like some of the other state plans, also raises a question about the proper use of tax-exempt financing. Why should a state offer what is already available in the form of the CollegeSure CD or other private sector instruments? The answer is that tax-exempt bonds would have a better after-tax rate of return in the state plan than in any private scheme. But that rate is better by virtue of a federal tax benefit provided through the use of tax-exempt financing. The state's financial obligation has in effect been shifted to the federal government. Tax-exempt bonds are supposed to be used for public purposes, and the widening definition by states of what constitutes a public purpose led a few years ago to a crackdown on the use of tax-exempt financing and the imposition of per capita limits on how much states can borrow.

In addition, the Massachusetts proposal calls for the issuance of small-denomination general obligation bonds. Such bonds are not often issued because bond underwriters believe the costs of administration do not justify the convenience offered to buyers of smaller denominations. The Commonwealth of Massachusetts does currently have a program in which it sells minibonds of $50, and these bonds certainly could be used for this purpose. But are there enough minibonds to fund a college savings program, and can the traditional reluctance of underwriters to sell small-denomination bonds be sufficiently overcome? A better approach might be for the state to establish a college savings fund in which parents and others could buy shares that in turn could be used to buy tax-exempt bonds. Such a fund mechanism could be used under either a tuition guarantee or straight savings approach.

The virtue of combining elements of savings and guarantee plans may also turn into a liability if some of the worst features of each are present. Like most guarantee plans the Massachusetts plan is complicated. Savings plans without a guarantee are generally much easier to understand and administer, but Massachusetts sacrifices simplicity and flexibility by incorporating a guarantee feature. Also, the partial guarantee of tuition under the Massachusetts approach possibly leaves participants unprotected on that part of their tuition that is not covered by the plan. The family who guarantees a part of its future tuition payments may find that the rest of its tuition bill has been increased to pay for the benefits of the guarantee.

The Massachusetts plan was signed into law in January 1990 and is to be administered by the Massachusetts Education Loan Authority. The fact that the plan incorporates elements of both savings and guarantee schemes increases the interest in seeing how the plan evolves during its implementation. It would not be surprising to discover other states or private organizations developing plans in the future that attempt to combine the best features of both.

Chapter Three

New Versions of the Traditional Student Aid Programs

Much of the innovative financing to emerge in recent years has focused on the tuition guarantee and savings plans discussed in chapter 2. But over the longer term more effort has gone into developing alternative forms of the traditional student aid programs of loans, grants, and work-study. Although this effort has normally not been in the limelight, a great deal of groundwork has been done on alternative loan programs for students and their parents, income-contingent loan repayment plans, incentives geared toward increasing the participation of economically disadvantaged students, merit-based aid, and the concept of linking student aid and public service.

Alternative Loan Programs

In the 1980s the Stafford loan program became the largest source of student financial aid in the United States. Its annual volume grew from $1 billion in the mid-1970s to roughly $10 billion in the late 1980s. The loan volume in this one program now represents two-fifths of the financial aid provided for students from all sources, which is up from less than one-tenth of all student aid in the mid-1970s. This growth in the use of loans has been a consequence of various circumstances, including the status of the program as a federal budget entitlement. The legal assurance that the full value of the interest subsidy and default payments will be received not only has encouraged lenders to participate in the program, but has also helped the program to grow at a time when funding for federal student aid programs that are subject to annual appropriations decisions has been restrained.

There is little doubt that the rapid growth of student loans over the past decade has helped to make postsecondary education a reality for millions of students. Roughly one-third of the students who attend college at least half time now borrow, compared with about one-tenth a decade ago. Loans have been especially important for students attending private colleges and universities, where prices are much higher than in the public sector. Thus in the 1980s the expanded use of loans played a critical role in enabling private sector institutions to maintain their share of enrollments at about one-quarter, after several decades of decline.

Loans have also been instrumental in the growth of proprietary (for-profit) trade schools. Although complete program data are not available, it appears that more than half the students at trade schools borrow Stafford loans and that they now constitute about one-third of all borrowers in the program. Enrollments in these schools have grown tremendously since the late 1970s, and it is inconceivable that such growth would have occurred without student loans.

The growth in the Stafford program has also brought increased attention and criticism. One problem is the expense of the program. Annual federal payments in the late 1980s have been roughly $3 billion, and if market interest rates increase, annual federal expenditures for Stafford loans in the future will easily top $5 billion. Federal costs for defaults alone are now close to $2 billion a year. On a long-term basis the federal costs for interest subsidies and guarantees against defaults range from 30 to 50 cents per dollar lent, depending on the interest rate. Another problem is the structure of the program, which provides lenders and other players with incentives to make more loans and larger loans because that will increase the federal interest payments they receive. There also continues to be too little incentive to prevent defaults before they occur; at present, none of the participants in the program, other than the federal government, bear much of the cost associated with default.

With the growth in the federal budget deficit, the search for savings in federal programs has intensified, and the Stafford program has been a frequent budget-cutting target. Administration budget proposals over the past decade have prominently listed it as one of the programs slated for reform, but Congress has rejected most proposals for large-scale change. Supporters of the program have successfully argued that, basically, it is working well and is too important a source of aid to endanger by changing the way it operates or by substantially reducing its level of subsidy.

Congress did agree to some changes in the 1980s: it imposed a 5 percent origination fee paid by borrowers that is used to offset federal interest costs somewhat, and it required students to demonstrate financial need (defined as costs of attendance minus family contribution and other resources) to be eligible to borrow. The Stafford program has also become the target of seemingly annual legislative changes designed to tighten its administrative machinery and thus produce modest savings. But the basic structure of the program remains intact. The legislative uneasiness about the growth in student loans can be seen in the decision by Congress in 1986 not to increase loan limits in the program as much as was previously planned or expected.

In contrast, funding for the other main federal loan program for students—Perkins loans (previously known as NDSL)—has remained relatively constant in nominal terms, thereby declining when adjusted for inflation. In the Perkins program, educational institutions act as lenders, using federal funds as their primary source of capital; participating colleges and universities provide 10 percent of the new loan capital. Loan repayments go into a revolving fund maintained by the institution for new loans. The long-term federal cost of Perkins loans is slightly lower than the cost of Stafford. The size of the subsidy that goes to borrowers through lower Perkins interest rates is more than offset by the fact that educational institutions do not receive special allowance interest payments from the federal government, as they do in Stafford loans. Despite this lower long-term cost, funding for Perkins loans has suffered, mainly because it is not a federal budget entitlement like Stafford loans. Federal capital contributions to the Perkins program appear in the budget as an expenditure when they are provided, whereas Stafford costs extend over the longer term, and most are hidden when the loan is made.

Among the proposals for overall federal budget reform are suggestions for changing the way the federal government accounts for its credit programs. Under one proposal, the subsidy value of federal loan programs would appear in the budget rather than the annual appropriations for such loans. Such a change would have an interesting effect on the comparative costs of Stafford and Perkins loans. The on-budget costs for GSL would increase relative to current practice, whereas Perkins loan costs would be reduced.

New Federal Loan Programs

Rather than consistently increase Stafford loan limits or provide larger appropriations for Perkins loans, Congress has authorized two alternative loan programs that offer a federal guarantee against default but carry little or none of the federal interest subsidies provided through Stafford. One of these programs is parent loans for undergraduate students (PLUS); its guarantee of private loans allows the parents of undergraduate students to spread some of the burden of paying for their children's college costs over a longer period of time. The other program, now called supplemental loans for students (SLS), provides nonsubsidized loans to graduate and professional school students and to undergraduates who are judged to be financially independent of their parents. The interest rate for both of these loan programs had been pegged at 12 percent, but legislation in 1986 changed them into variable interest rate loans tied to annual changes in the rate for one-year Treasury bills.

Loan volume in the PLUS program has grown relatively slowly despite parents' frequent pleas for help in financing their children's college costs. One reason for this slow growth may be that when rates were pegged at 12 percent, many parents were able to get a better deal through nonfederal loans, such as home equity loans from banks or programs sponsored by states or institutions. Moving to variable interest rates should help overcome this

obstacle, and volume is expanding. Loans guaranteed in the
PLUS program were in excess of $500 million in fiscal 1988, or
one-twentieth of total federal loan volume in that year, but double
the PLUS loan volume in fiscal 1986.

Growth in the SLS program also lagged until recently, but
then it jumped from less than $300 million in fiscal 1986 to more
than $700 million in fiscal 1987. In fiscal 1988 SLS loan volumes
approached $2 billion, which was almost triple the fiscal 1987
level and more than five times the fiscal 1986 volume. The
primary reason for this remarkable growth is that SLS, which
had previously been limited mainly to students in graduate and
professional schools, is now being used by a growing number of
students in proprietary schools, who today account for well over
half of all borrowers in the program. The paperwork and eligibility
requirements for these loans are much less stringent than for
Stafford loans, and the annual loan limits are $4,000 for first-
year students, in contrast to the $2,625 available to these students
in the Stafford program. As a result, many of these new SLS
borrowers apparently did not borrow in the Stafford program at
all, but instead were using SLS as their only source of student
loans.

The growing number of proprietary school students in the SLS
program is of great concern because proprietary schools have
accounted for a disproportionate share of defaults in the Stafford
program. Therefore, the default costs in the program are likely
to mushroom. Moreover, it is troubling to see a group of predominantly low-income students shifting or being encouraged to shift
from a subsidized lending program to a largely unsubsidized one.
Some remedial federal legislation was enacted in 1988 and 1989,
including a requirement that borrowers must first apply for a
Stafford loan before being eligible for an SLS and restrictions on
how much first-year students can borrow in the program. These
requirements will reduce some of the abuse in the program and
will have some effect on the volume of loans. But more restrictions
should be placed on the use of SLS by proprietary school students,
including possibly a total prohibition. At the same time, it would
be desirable to extend eligibility to financially dependent college

students who are no longer eligible for Stafford loans because of their financial circumstances.

Nonfederal Loan Alternatives

Although most of the proposed student loan reforms have thus far been rejected by Congress, publicity about the proposed cutbacks and the lack of an increase in the program's loan maximums have encouraged roughly half the states to develop loan programs of their own. Approximately $500 million in loans are awarded annually through these alternative state programs. Initially, many states financed these loan programs through tax-exempt bonds, but now they can use this instrument only to a limited degree. Consequently, the growth of these state programs has begun to slow down, and the search is on for other forms of financing, including some from private sources.

Many student loan programs have also been developed by colleges and universities, especially private institutions, where tuitions are much higher and concerns about financing are that much greater. These institutional plans have taken many forms. In several instances consortia of institutions have been formed to sponsor a loan program. The largest and most publicized of these is the SHARE program, in which a group of thirty private colleges and universities sponsored a loan program for parents and students at their institutions. Another consortium effort, ConSern loans for education, uses tax-exempt financing to provide loans for parents and students at participating institutions. Professional school associations in medicine, dentistry, and law have each developed loan programs for students attending the schools they represent. In other cases, institutions have signed agreements with insurance companies to provide loans combined with insurance for the parents of their students. Still other institutions have established their own programs, using either tax-exempt bonds, endowments, or private funds.

There are also a growing number of private sector loan programs for students, and especially their parents, that are provided through banks, insurance companies, and other sources of capital. The growing interest in these private efforts is in large part a result of the perceived erosion in the adequacy of the federal loan programs, or of increased restrictions in eligibility for federally subsidized loans. When the interest rate in the federal alternative programs was pegged at 12 percent, many students and their families turned to private or institutional loans, where the market-based rates were lower. One such program is being sponsored by the Chamber of Commerce and run by the ConSern organization. Loans are financed with commercial paper and are made to the employees of organizations that belong to the Chamber of Commerce. Most banks and many financial institutions, recognizing the concerns of their customers, have established student or parent loan programs of their own.

Efforts have been made to convert these private sector student and parent loans (as well as many of the institution-based plans) into home equity loans, since the 1986 tax legislation allows deductions for interest on education loans only if they are secured through home equity. In at least one respect, however, a trend toward the use of home equity loans introduces additional ine-quities into the current tax system. The mortgage interest deduction, which already favors those who own their homes, will probably become even more of a tax sanctuary for better-off families, who will use this provision as a means of paying for college.

The alternative state, institutional, and private sector loan programs that have evolved in recent years differ in some significant ways from the federal programs. They usually require a credit check of the borrower and sometimes the provision of collateral, unlike the federal programs, where the federal guar-antee substitutes for credit checks and collateral requirements. Interest rates are usually set at market levels and are therefore higher than the subsidized rates in the federal programs. Also, the state, institutional, and private loan programs by and large have established loan limits that are higher than those in the federal programs.

The development of nonfederal loan alternatives should in general be viewed as a healthy trend: states, institutions, and the private sector are seeking to meet a growing demand for loans created by new restrictions in the traditional federal programs coupled with continuing increases in college costs. But the introduction of many new loan programs on top of the existing ones adds complexity to what was already a complex system. Students and their families must now apply to many more sources for assistance. Moreover, for many borrowers, no mechanism exists to consolidate their nonfederal loans into a single repayment instrument. Future modifications in these nonfederal loan efforts should focus on these concerns.

Income-Contingent Repayment Proposals

Another troubling question about the increased volume of student loans is whether the borrowers will be able to repay their obligations once they complete their education. Even though the default rate has not substantially increased over time, the larger loan volume and the consequent rapid growth in federal payments for defaults lend credence to concerns about excessive repayment levels.

In addition, mounting debt burdens may be having an adverse effect on students' educational, career, and personal decisions. Although the available data suggest that the debt burdens of most students are still within reasonable limits, some students may begin to wonder whether the benefits of the education are worth the additional debt they might incur and whether they shouldn't enter a career in which they can make enough to pay off their student loans. The repayment burden may even influence their decisions on whom to marry and whether to have children.

Income-contingent repayments are the solution most often suggested to prevent repayment problems from reaching excessive levels. The idea of a system in which the repayment of student loans is based on the incomes of borrowers once they complete their education is not new. Milton Friedman first proposed it in 1945. Since then, the idea has resurfaced periodically in articles and reports. In 1967 President Lyndon Johnson's Science Advisory Committee, chaired by Jerold Zacharias, recommended that the government create a national student loan bank in which repay-

ments would be geared to a borrower's income. John Silber of
Boston University has pushed for income-contingent loans as
part of his proposed tuition advance fund. Income-contingent loan
proposals have also been offered in the last two reauthorizations
of the Higher Education Act.

The Reagan administration was the first one to implement the
concept through its income-contingent loan (ICL) program. It
successfully lobbied for a pilot program involving ten colleges
and universities offering income-contingent loans through the
existing institution-based Perkins loan program. Borrowers repay
on a scale that slides with their income and the amount of debt.
Those with a low income and low debt pay as little as 5 percent
of their income, but most borrowers in the program pay the top
rate of 12 percent. No government subsidy is provided. Interest
rates charged to borrowers are set above the Treasury's cost of
funds. In years when the borrower's income-related repayment
is less than the interest on the remaining principal, the unpaid
interest is to be added to the principal. The plan does not provide
for any loan cancellation; borrowers would not be excused from
their repayment obligations over the course of their lifetime
except for reasons of death or disability.

Although the ICL is advertised as an income-contingent program, the total amount owed or repaid does not vary with one's
income. Strictly speaking, an income-contingent approach would
ask higher-income borrowers to repay a higher proportion of the
amount they initially borrowed than lower-income borrowers do.
What varies with income under the ICL plan is the size of the
annual payments or the length of repayment. As a result, some
analysts describe this as an income-sensitive rather than an
income-contingent arrangement.

The existence of a cross subsidy between borrowers with high
and low incomes is what allows a truly income-contingent plan
to be self-financing. But this subsidy may result in adverse
selection, since borrowers who believe their future incomes will
be high may be reluctant to participate. To prevent adverse
selection, Reagan administration officials opted for a program
that did not require higher-income borrowers to repay more than
they borrowed plus interest. Since no penalty is imposed on

borrowers for having a high income, there is no particular reason for students who believe their future incomes will be high not to participate in the ICL program.

Some observers have suggested that adverse selection was the primary reason that previous income-contingent student loan experiments at Yale and Duke universities foundered. Yale officials contend that adverse selection was not why they discontinued the plan. They note that provisions in the Yale plan that allowed borrowers to prepay, or "buy out," their repayment obligation appear to have minimized the number of students with high-income expectations who did not participate. Yale officials contend, instead, that the plan was dropped because of the greater availability of federal loans in the late 1970s. Moreover, the Yale plan apparently was never intended as anything more than an experiment. It is significant that Yale, for all its endowment, did not believe it could support the capital requirements of a full-fledged loan program.

In defending their ICL plan, Reagan officials also made the typical arguments in favor of income-contingent repayments. The basic concept is very appealing. Borrowers repay their loans on the basis of what they earn once they complete their education rather than at an amortized level that is unrelated to their earning capacity. This logic has apparently convinced the Bush administration to continue proposing expansions of the program.

But the Reagan-Bush ICL approach suffers from several drawbacks that have dogged previous income-contingent loan proposals. It is complex, and the way it operates and the effects it produces are difficult to understand. Like most income-contingent plans, the ICL requires all borrowers in the program to submit income tax information. Otherwise it would ask the IRS to furnish this information to the educational institution (which would then be able to keep track of the income of its alumni in a rather threatening way). The participation of the IRS has long been a sticking point in debates over income-contingent loans, in part because the IRS itself does not want to be involved.

The ICL program is also flawed in some ways not shared by other income-contingent approaches. The 12 percent of annual income that most borrowers are required to repay is a level of debt service that would, in most cases, disqualify the student loan borrower from obtaining a mortgage. By not containing any provision to excuse borrowers from their obligation, short of death or disability, some number of borrowers whose incomes are already low will in addition be saddled with a lifetime of student loan indebtedness. Finally, the income-contingent feature applies only to a relatively small share of total federal student loans; borrowers in the much larger Stafford, SLS, Perkins, and other federal loan programs are not afforded this repayment option.

Modifications in the Income-Contingent Concept

Some analysts have suggested ways of improving the income-contingent concept. For example, Robert Reischauer has proposed that student loans be transformed into a social insurance program and that the social security trust fund be used as both the source of capital and the avenue of repayment for student loans.[1] Under this proposal students would be able to pay for a portion of their college costs by borrowing from the social security trust fund. Borrowers would repay in the form of additional payroll tax payments over the course of their lifetimes. Reischauer estimates that an additional one-quarter of 1 percent in the tax rate per $1,000 borrowed would be enough to ensure a rate of return to the trust fund commensurate with current yields.

This approach would use the social security trust fund instead of private funds or federal appropriations as the source of capital, and the payroll tax would substitute for the income tax as the means of repayment. Virtually all workers now pay into social security, so that the issue of noncoverage is no longer significant. Those borrowers who do not remain active in the labor force for their entire working lives, such as nonworking spouses, might not fully repay their loans. But this could be justified as a

1. Robert D. Reischauer, "HELP: A Student Loan Program for the Twenty-First Century," in Lawrence E. Gladieux, ed., *Radical Reform or Incremental Change?* (New York: College Board, 1989), pp. 33–56.

reasonable component of an enlightened family policy. Most other income-contingent plans use joint incomes to measure the capacity to repay, whereas the Reischauer plan would have each borrower repay on the basis of his or her own income and debt levels, and in this way would reduce the problem of a negative dowry for two-borrower couples. Nor would it require student loan repayments from noncovered income from capital and other nonwage income, as would most other income-contingent plans.

Michael Dukakis in his 1988 presidential campaign picked up on the Reischauer approach in his student tuition and repayment system (STARS) proposal, which called for loan repayments through the payroll taxes. But the Dukakis campaign staff, concerned about the political reaction to opening up the social security trust fund, altered the Reischauer plan in at least two significant ways: they would have allowed banks and other private sector lenders to continue as the source of student loan capital, and they would have used these income-contingent loans to supplement rather than replace current programs. But these changes, which came about mostly in response to political pressure, detract substantially from the logic of the original Reischauer plan.

One question that has been raised about the Reischauer plan is whether it is appropriate to extend the concept of social insurance to student loans. Notwithstanding the current state of affairs in higher education finance, it may still be reaching too far to say that paying for college belongs in the same category as the national concerns that social insurance covers, such as unemployment, welfare, and health care.

Moreover, although the problem of student loan defaults certainly needs to be addressed, repaying loans through the tax system to ensure collection may be a policy overreaction. The vast majority of borrowers are currently repaying on the traditional basis, so that it is worth asking whether these reliable repayers should be subjected to a radically different repayment burden in order to solve the default problem. There are other, much less radical, changes that would relieve the federal government of paying for the costs of defaults. For example, all student borrowers could be charged an insurance fee that would be sufficient to pay for the anticipated costs of default.

Another possibility would be to make income-based repayments available only to those borrowers whose student loan obligations exceed their ability to repay once they complete their education. Under this kind of income-contingent approach, which might be termed low-income insurance, borrowers whose incomes were not sufficient to meet their debt service could apply for assistance in the form of alternative repayment arrangements. For example, the term of repayment might be extended beyond the conventional ten-year period, or a graduated repayment schedule might be used in which annual repayments are smaller than the amortized level of repayment in the early years of repayment and larger in the later years, when the borrower will probably have more resources. Both these adjustments are already available for those borrowers with large debts who are eligible to consolidate their student loans, but not for borrowers of smaller amounts, who are more likely to default. Or borrowers could pay a stated portion of their income. This last option would differ from a full-scale income-contingent plan in that only those borrowers with low incomes relative to their debts would participate, whereas in a typical income-contingent plan all borrowers must pay according to their incomes, even those who can afford to pay in a more conventional fashion.

Most observers now agree that a principal cause of student loan defaults is that many borrowers simply do not have sufficient incomes to repay their student loans when they finish their educational program. Many defaulters are not so much unwilling to repay as they are unable to repay. Rather than being tagged and hounded as a defaulter, those borrowers with high debts relative to their incomes need some systematic means of making their repayments manageable. Low-income insurance would be one possible solution.

The concept of low-income insurance can also be tied in with some of the proposals that would link public service with student aid, which are discussed at the end of this chapter. Some of those proposals would forgive the loans of borrowers who entered designated professions such as teaching, or who served in the

Peace Corps or similar programs. In effect, low-income insurance is a form of loan forgiveness that affords protection for student borrowers who choose to enter lower-paying positions because of a desire to perform public service. Low-income insurance differs from loan forgiveness, however, in that it also helps those borrowers for whom low income is not a choice.

A few educational institutions and states have already put into effect programs of low-income insurance. At least a dozen law schools now offer their graduates the option of repaying their loans on the basis of their income if they choose to enter lower-paying public service careers. Typically, the law school will make some form of financial commitment to the students who enter such positions, either by buying the loans of the students and establishing a new repayment schedule, or by assuming that part of the repayment which exceeds a certain percentage of a borrower's income. For example, under Harvard Law School's low-income protection plan (LIPP), the school will pay a graduate's entire law school debt if he or she accepts a law-related position that pays less than $20,000 adjusted for inflation over time. Those graduates earning $20,000 to $30,000 a year are expected to pay 6 percent of their income, and the school will pay the rest of the student's annual repayment obligation. Similar plans have also been adopted at a small number of business and medical schools.

Among the states, Minnesota has established a low-income protection program for students in the health professions. Under its graduated repayment income protection (GRIP) plan, the state helps consolidate a student's various loan obligations and establishes extended and graduated repayment terms. If the borrower's annual repayment obligation then exceeds 10 percent of income, the state pays the amount of the annual repayment obligation in excess of 10 percent. The plan has been successful enough for the state to consider extending it to other fields of study.

In a way, though, these first efforts at providing low-income insurance have been aimed at the wrong population of borrowers. Most of these programs are for students in graduate and professional schools who may choose or be forced to take positions that are relatively low paying for their profession, but by most reasonable standards are still good jobs. The borrowers that the existing efforts miss are the ones who have low incomes by any standard. They have borrowed to get a chance to improve their economic situation, but the bet has not paid off in the form of a well-paying job. Now they are stuck with a student debt that they cannot repay. These are the borrowers for whom low-income insurance is vital.

Ironically, an informal form of low-income insurance is already in effect in every state. After the lenders in the Stafford program have performed the requisite "due diligence" in collecting on a delinquent student loan, they turn over the paper to the state guaranty agency in exchange for reimbursement. When the guaranty agency receives federal reinsurance on the default claim, it generally holds on to the bad paper. Federal law then encourages the agency to collect from the defaulter by allowing it to retain 30 percent of what it collects as an incentive for collection. Guaranty agencies now collect several hundred million dollars annually through this mechanism.

By and large, the defaulters who resume repayments are not those who have been thumbing their noses at the system. Instead, they are typically the borrowers who simply did not have enough income to make payments on their loan. In many of these cases, it is easier for the bank to turn over the loan to the guaranty agency than to work out an alternative repayment schedule. When the agency contacts these borrowers, many of them agree to set up partial repayment schedules until they can get back on their feet. Some states—Illinois is one example—have developed extensive programs along these lines. What is unfortunate is that we force these borrowers into the default category and give them a bad name and a hard time when we should be trying to give them a hand. The current system also does not minimize federal costs, since the federal government pays off the guaranty agency first and then receives only a part of what the agency collects from the borrower. It would be better if the state guaranty agencies were provided an incentive to delay making a reimbursement claim with the federal government until they had tried to establish an alternative payment schedule with the defaulting borrower.

Assured Access for Low-Income and Minority Students

Among the most troubling trends in higher education has been the recent lack of progress in improving the participation rates of low-income and minority students. This drop has frequently been ascribed to the decline in the availability of student aid for these students. But the facts may not bear out this theory. Although the maximum levels of aid have not kept pace with inflation, sufficient federal, state, institutional, and private funds are available so that most impoverished students certainly can afford to attend low-tuition public institutions if they so desire. Even so, participation rates among target groups of students have not improved appreciably, and may have declined. Consequently, a number of efforts have been designed to improve access for these target groups, primarily through a combination of promises to pay the costs of college attendance and the provision of support services.

The "I Have a Dream" Concept

In 1981 Eugene Lang, a wealthy industrialist and philanthropist, was preparing to address the graduating sixth-grade class from the East Harlem elementary school in New York City, which he had attended half a century before. The student body that day was in some ways significantly different from the one in which he had been a member. Most of the students he addressed were from minority groups and were living in an area that was severely economically depressed. But in some ways it was the same—most of the students were from poor families and many of their parents were recent immigrants. Rather than stick to his prepared text, Lang decided at the last minute to make a promise to the students: if they graduated from high school and were accepted at college, he would pay their way.

What Lang ultimately agreed to do was to make up the difference between the amount of government grant aid that the students would be eligible to receive and the attendance costs at the institution that accepted them. Thus Lang's students could rely on a full package of grant assistance wherever they were accepted. At the time, Lang calculated that an investment of roughly $200,000 plus interest until the class reached college age would be sufficient to cover the payments necessary to make up the difference between what the students would be eligible to receive through federal, state, and institutional student aid programs and their costs of attendance.

But Lang's concept as it evolved went much further than the provision of some additional financial aid. Perhaps its most important component was the promise to provide an environment of support for students as they proceeded through junior and senior high school, to allow them to believe that going on to college was in fact a reality. For Lang's class of sixth graders, the support was provided through a house set up in the neighborhood to serve as a center of student activities. Since the students attended high schools located all over the city, the center was the place where much of the tutoring and other support services occurred for the group, and where the students could gather to talk among themselves and to meet with their mentors and tutors. A personal touch was also provided by Lang, who met with the students individually at his office to hear about the progress they were making toward the goal of high school graduation and college admission.

In the many speeches he now is asked to give on the subject, Lang points out that the promise of a college education does not mean anything unless it is communicated in a useful and intelligent way. Providing support services and showing that somebody cares are two important ways to make that promise more real for this set of students. It is also critical that it be made early enough in the student's educational career to make a difference. Promising a college education to a sixteen-year-old about to drop out is not likely to meet with as much success as telling it to the same student in junior high school.

The results of the Lang experiment have been astounding. Of the class of sixty-one sixth graders that he addressed, only one failed to complete high school, and more than half applied and were admitted to a postsecondary educational program. It would be reasonable to expect that in a control group of sixth graders from a similar type of school who were not offered the same incentive, the proportion who complete high school and go on to college would be about one out of ten.

The Lang experiment has not been going on long enough to determine how much effect it has had on the persistence of students to complete college. And the experiment may be contaminated by the attention that has been paid to Lang's beneficiaries; the students may be doing better simply because they are in the spotlight. But the impact on access and the enrollment decisions made by Eugene Lang's students and the partial results from other similar efforts are enough to recommend this kind of approach as possibly an important strategy for the future. The success of his initial group of students has led Eugene Lang to establish the "I Have a Dream" Foundation, through which he encourages other philanthropists to set up similar programs. More than a hundred people had established similar programs in their own communities by the end of 1988.

A number of cities and universities have developed assured access programs that either predate Lang's speech in 1981 or have evolved contemporaneously in the 1980s. In Cleveland, Ohio, for example, a scholarship program began in 1967 as a partnership of local businesses, foundations, the school system, and local colleges and universities. It provides local high schools with academic and financial aid counselors as well as "last dollar" scholarships to fill the gaps in state and federal aid programs for a portion of the city's economically disadvantaged students. Since the program's inception, the proportion of Cleveland public school students enrolling in postsecondary education has increased from one-eighth to over one-half. Boston's Action Center for Educational Services and Scholarships (ACCESS), which began in 1984, is another example of a partnership along these lines. A dozen other cities including Baltimore, Philadelphia, and Atlanta have started similar partnership programs that raise funds for inner-city college-bound youth. The success of these efforts strongly indicates that public and private concern at the community level is one approach that should be expanded.

In addition, a number of institutions (including Xavier, Boston,

and Syracuse universities) have made a commitment to provide
full scholarships for students in target high schools in their
communities as well as additional support services through
faculty-sharing arrangements and other measures.

The success of these efforts has pointed up three glaring
shortcomings of current government programs. First, the amount
of aid they provide is generally far short of what is needed to
meet the total costs of attendance at many institutions for a
group of students who cannot realistically consider borrowing.
The current Pell grant maximum award is not large enough to
meet the average total costs of attendance at any type of higher
education institution, including community colleges. When the
Pell award is combined with state grant assistance, the amount
is still insufficient to cover the full costs of attendance at many
public institutions and virtually all private colleges and universities. Economically disadvantaged students are left with the
option of borrowing or working, both of which are likely to have
a negative effect on their rates of participation in higher education.

The experience with the assured access approach also suggests
that providing student aid without sufficient support services is
a strategy doomed to failure. Nevertheless, few policy debates
pay adequate attention to support services such as tutoring and
counseling. The federal TRIO programs do provide such services
through programs such as upward bound and talent search, but
TRIO has been chronically underfunded. Currently, fewer than
one in ten students eligible for TRIO receives assistance through
these programs. Furthermore, most of the funding that is available goes to institutions that have successful programs, with the
result that other institutions have less incentive to improve the
support services that they provide on their own campuses.

A third shortcoming of the current system of student aid is
that it fails to give early notification and assurance of aid. Eugene
Lang may not have realized it, but when he threw away his
prepared comments and made his promise to the students, he
was putting into action the original premise and the promise of
the federal Pell grant program, when it was enacted as the basic
grants program in the early 1970s. The idea at that time was

that students should be informed of their eligibility for federal student aid beginning as early as the ninth grade as a way of raising their aspirations. It was also assumed that sufficient aid would be provided to allow the lowest-income students to gain access to some form of postsecondary educational training.

This initial promise of the Pell grant legislation has not been realized. One reason is that the notion of a simple system and early notice was never incorporated into the program design. Instead, the application process has been about as complicated as the rest of the student aid system, which is to say it is not quite as difficult as filling out the full range of income tax forms, but far more complicated than the 1040 EZ. More important, no effort has been made to tell students in the ninth grade that aid is available or roughly how much aid they can get. Instead, the program has operated on a short-term basis, with funding never decided until shortly before the school year begins. Also, eligibility standards have been subject to frequent changes, which tend to give students a poor impression of the program's reliability and predictability.

Too often, information on the availability of student aid is not given to the students who need aid the most. This is a major shortcoming of the current student aid system. What Eugene Lang did was to provide that information and that aid directly and in a credible way for the students who needed it most and for whom student aid is primarily intended. The experience with assured access efforts thus far suggests that a program in which sufficient funds are combined with a personal touch and long-term commitment can raise the participation of disadvantaged students in a meaningful way.

The question is, can this be done and institutionalized at a governmental level, so that it is a viable option for a much broader range of the "at-risk" population? The current efforts are too random, and it is unlikely that the amount of aid provided through a network of philanthropists and a smattering of cities and institutions will ever be sufficient to make a large dent in the underlying problem. Ultimately, the necessary level of resources can probably be obtained only from federal or state governments.

New York's Liberty Scholarships

States are the most logical candidates for a governmental approach to assured access: the range of institutions is large enough to provide students with a real choice, and the base of tax revenues is broad enough to provide an adequate level of resources. The federal government, on the other hand, is probably too far removed from the school systems and the colleges and universities to afford the personal touch necessary for the success of a venture of this kind.

In New York State, spurred in large part by the success of Eugene Lang's "class," Governor Mario Cuomo in 1988 proposed the Liberty scholarship program as a prominent part of his legislative agenda for meeting the needs of the "Decade of the Child." Under Cuomo's initial proposal, seventh-grade students would qualify for assistance if they were eligible for the school lunch program, where the current income eligibility standard is 130 percent of the poverty level. If these students completed high school and were admitted to a New York State institution, they would then be eligible for an award that equaled the difference between the costs of attending a public institution within the state and the amount of aid they were eligible to receive under the federal Pell grant program and the state's tuition assistance program (TAP). Students who were admitted to a private institution within the state would receive the same amount.

In July 1988 the Liberty scholarship program was enacted into law, but it varied somewhat from the initial Cuomo proposal. The program now on the books, which will go into effect during the 1991-92 academic year, will cover only nontuition expenses, as it is assumed that the state's existing tuition assistance program (TAP) meets the full tuition at New York public institutions. Students from families with incomes below $18,000 will be eligible for the maximum award, and awards will be reduced one dollar for every three dollars of income above $18,000. At the same time, the maximum TAP award levels were substantially increased to help pay for rising tuitions at private institutions within the state.

The legislation also included a Liberty partnership provision in which competitive grants will be made to New York colleges and universities and community-based organizations beginning in 1989-90. The purpose of the partnership grants is to provide more one-on-one mentoring and counseling services to prevent dropout at elementary and secondary schools. The partnership measure underscores the importance that the legislation places on the theme of dropout prevention.

The changes made in the governor's proposal as it moved through the legislative process represent both improvements and setbacks to the initial plan. The Liberty partnerships are a big step forward; they give recognition to the critical need for additional support services as well as more financial aid if the students are to complete their high school education and be ready for college. But the fact that the early notice and identification of eligible students has been downplayed or eliminated is disappointing. This is a mistake similar to that made during the early implementation of the Pell grant program, when early notice and simplicity were sacrificed to make the program fit into the mold of the other traditional student aid programs.

Several states—including West Virginia, Washington, and Florida—have established more modest scholarship and awareness programs aimed at the most economically disadvantaged students. A number of other states are looking into the possibility of emulating New York's Liberty scholarship approach as a way to raise the college participation of low-income and minority students. These states should draw on the lessons learned thus far in New York and from Eugene Lang and other philanthropists about the need for early notice, the importance of support services, and the desirability of providing a full measure of grant assistance for students for whom loans and work are likely to continue to represent a substantial obstacle to their participation in higher education.

There should also be a recognition that some states could use an assured access approach more than others. For example, states that have metropolitan areas with large concentrations of at-risk youth are more likely to need an early intervention strategy than more rural states. Similarly, for states with relatively large numbers of private sector institutions, an assured access program will be more expensive (to cover the costs of private institutions) than for states with mostly lower-priced public institutions.

Providing Merit-Based Aid
to Needy Students

Up to the mid-1950s a large percentage of all student financial aid was provided on a merit basis. Educational institutions competed for students by offering the largest and most attractive aid packages to the best students, regardless of their financial need. Foundation and other philanthropic support was also awarded largely on a competitive basis. In addition, the aid package that students were offered varied greatly from school to school, since no standardized procedure was available to determine a family's financial need. These disparities led several dozen institutions in the mid-1950s to join together in developing a common procedure for establishing need and in forming the College Scholarship Service.

In the more than three decades since then, financial need has become the standard determinant of most student aid awards at colleges and universities. All the states have established at least one grant program that is based on a student's financial need. Although the federal government adheres to the merit principle for most of the fellowship and other aid it provides to graduate school students, federal aid to undergraduates continues to be built overwhelmingly on the principle of financial need.

Since 1980, however, the notion of merit-based aid has experienced a resurgence. A number of states have enacted small programs of aid that are based on students' academic achievements or other measures not related to financial need. In 1986 the federal government also enacted a program of merit aid called Byrd scholarships, after its chief Senate sponsor, Robert C. Byrd (Democrat of West Virginia), which provides aid for the best high school students in each congressional district.

Colleges and universities are the principal providers of merit-based aid. Typically, this aid is provided within the context of the need-based aid system in that students must have some degree of need in order to qualify for the merit-based aid. However, some amount of merit-based aid is provided for students with no demonstrated financial need in the form of assistance targeted for athletes, musicians, and students with other high-priority attributes. Some also comes from restricted endowment funds that are limited to designated types of students without regard to their financial need. Although no reliable data on aid from institutions are available at present, the prevailing sense is that most of the aid they provide continues to be need-based, but that merit-based aid as a proportion of institutionally funded aid has grown over the past decade.

There is also an implicit component of merit built into the current system of need-based financial aid. Highly selective institutions tend to be the most desirable, to cost the most, and to give the most need-based aid to their students. To the extent that the best students attend these institutions, they receive more need-based aid. Institutions also tend to provide more attractive financial aid packages to their better students while remaining within the confines of the financial aid principles. Two students with equal need and unequal abilities are likely to receive different aid packages: the better student will typically receive more grant aid and less loan aid than the other student.

Several factors may account for the recent increase in merit aid. One is the decline in the size of the traditional college-age group, which has increased the competition among educational institutions for students. The competition for students in the early 1950s is what led to the development of needs analysis, and it seems that the growing competition for a declining number of traditional college-age students in the 1980s led to a degree of undercutting in the need-based principles that held sway in the three previous decades.

In recent years there have also been more expressions of concern about the decline in the quality of education that American students are receiving. Although most of this criticism has been leveled at elementary and secondary school education, some of it applies to postsecondary education as well. This concern about quality has often been translated into a desire to award more aid on the basis of merit as a means of encouraging greater educational achievement. The emergence of competitiveness as an issue of national concern has also contributed to the call for better quality because being more competitive is often equated with the need to improve quality.

Competitiveness is really a two-sided issue, since our national productivity cannot be improved unless we increase the overall number of well-educated citizens and not focus resources only on the very best students. For this reason, a large-scale shift toward more merit-based aid at the expense of need-based aid may not be salutary for the nation's competitiveness or its general well-being. We may do more damage to the deteriorating quality of American education if the goals of equity and opportunity are further sacrificed by focusing more resources on the best students. Providing funds to good students who are not needy can be an inefficient activity, since the additional resources may have little or no effect on the behavior of those students, while the larger potential of needy students will be neglected.

What makes sense, instead, is to direct a portion of student aid funds to the highly qualified students who also need financial assistance. This could be accomplished through student aid programs that select students on the basis of merit, however measured, but in which the amount of aid provided is based on a student's financial need. That is how many of the national merit programs work. Some programs at the state level are also provided in this manner, but this is the exception rather than the rule. Also, much of the aid that educational institutions provide is in effect delivered on this principle, since institutions tend to provide the best aid packages—more grants, fewer loans— to the best students who fall within a particular category of financial need.

Merging need-based and merit-based principles for a portion of aid can be justified on at least two grounds. First, it would reward those students who achieve the most, which should have a beneficial effect in raising the quality of a student's effort. A system that is based entirely on need—with no focus on merit— to some extent serves as a disincentive for greater striving on the part of the students. More important, a program based both on need and on merit could directly address the policy concern that high-ability students from lower-income families are still much less likely to attend college than students of equal ability who come from wealthier families. To the extent that the current need-based student aid programs have not successfully addressed this long-standing problem, a merit-based program in which the amount of aid provided is based on need would seem to be a worthwhile experiment.

Linking Student Aid with Community, Public, or National Service

Aid has been connected with service as far back as government student aid programs can be traced. In the 1930s the federal government operated a small work-study program in cooperation with the states to help depression-era students pay for their college expenses. By far the largest federal student aid program was service related: the GI Bill enabled millions of returning veterans from three wars to pay for their college education. The Economic Opportunity Act of 1964 established a pilot work-study program for economically disadvantaged college students. In 1965 this pilot program was incorporated into the student aid structure as the college work-study program in the Higher Education Act.

In the early 1970s GI Bill benefits for students in postsecondary education averaged $5 billion a year and made up half or more of all the student aid provided from all sources. During that time the college work-study program was a prominent feature of the federal campus-based programs. Since 1980, however, the linkage to service has become a decidedly smaller component of federal student aid. GI Bill expenditures declined as the number of veterans eligible to use these benefits decreased. In the late 1970s grant assistance grew rapidly, and work-study fell as a proportion of all aid provided. In the 1980s work-study declined further as a percentage of all aid, whereas loan assistance grew. In the late 1980s veterans' benefits and work-study combined constituted less than 5 percent of the total student aid provided.

Although the proportion of student aid provided in return for service has declined over time, the number of service opportunities has grown, especially in recent years. More than one hundred college presidents now belong to Campus Compact, a coalition that encourages colleges to provide greater volunteer opportunities for their students and that seeks federal and state support for policies and programs that encourage more students to perform service. The New York City Volunteer Corps, which links inner-city youth with service in the schools and in the community, is an example of what can be done at the local level. The California Conservation Corps, reminiscent of the depression-era Civilian Conservation Corps (CCC), provides outdoor service opportunities for young people within the state. Altogether, perhaps twenty to thirty thousand people annually benefit from the service opportunities that are currently provided.

A number of recent proposals would renew and enhance the connection between student aid and the performance of service in order to promote greater participation in community, public, or national service activities. It is difficult to generalize about these proposals, however, because they flow from a great variety of concerns, ranging from the apparent lack of interest on the part of many high school and college students in voluntary endeavors to the growing reliance on loans to pay for college costs and the impact that this reliance on credit may be having on the educational and career choices of borrowers. Some of these proposals also emphasize the desirability of involving Americans in public service and voluntary activities throughout their lives. In addition, national service proposals have been put forth as an alternative to the military draft so that young Americans can choose between military service and volunteer work.

Encouraging Voluntary Student Service

A growing cadre of educators and others have expressed concern that American students at all levels no longer have the commitment to volunteerism that helped this nation to grow. They worry about the isolation, the lethargy, and the lack of commitment they see in many students. To combat these trends, many educational leaders have been encouraging schools to develop programs that would involve students in volunteer activities in the community. As a result of these pressures, many high schools now offer service programs, which take a variety of forms. Some schools provide academic credit for such activities, whereas others do not. The services provided cover the gambit from health care to education to community conservation.

The value of volunteerism has been debated in the colleges for basically the same reasons as in the high schools: an apparent decline in interest in volunteer activities, growing cynicism among students about the value of volunteer work, and student preoccupation with activities that have monetary returns. To combat these attitudes, a handful of colleges—including Berea, Mount St. Mary's, and Alverno—have made performance of service one of their graduation requirements. At most institutions, however, service remains a voluntary activity. The establishment of the Campus Compact is another manifestation of the growth in campus-based concern about the absence of volunteerism.

Some linkage already exists between the rules of student aid programs and student service efforts. For example, the college work-study program has been modified so that funds may be used for service opportunities on and off campus. However, the connection between these service efforts and financial aid is by and large a weak one. The whole notion of volunteer work can be undermined by efforts that compensate students for activities that are supposed to be voluntary. In any case, student service efforts should probably not be thought of as a financing mechanism. Perhaps they belong more appropriately in the category of curriculum development and enhancement.

Careers in Public Service

Another reason behind the efforts to link public service and student aid is that fewer college graduates seem interested in participating in careers in the public or nonprofit sectors. This decline may be related to several factors: the growing debt of students and their consequent need to choose higher-paying jobs that will allow them to repay that debt; the elimination of the military draft and its effect on the decision calculus of college-age males; and the much discussed shift in society's goals from a desire for psychic compensation in the workplace to a desire for monetary recompense.

One possible indication of the shift in values is the fact that a growing proportion of college students are obtaining degrees in fields of study that are thought to lead to better-paying jobs. Between 1973-74 and 1983-84, for example, the number of bachelor's degrees awarded in business and management increased by about 75 percent, the increase in engineering was about 70 percent, and degrees in computer and information sciences multiplied sevenfold. By contrast, bachelor's degrees awarded in the humanities fell by one-quarter, social science degrees declined by two-fifths, and degrees awarded in education were cut in half.[2]

Similar trends have also been evident among students earning advanced degrees. A number of observers have fretted about this greater "career orientation" in the selection of majors as a sign that society no longer appreciates the value of a liberal arts education and a humanistic existence. According to other observers, these trends could be a sign that our economic competitiveness is improving. As in many areas of public policy, all goals do not lead to a single set of policies.

If we wish to combat the trend toward vocationalism in the selection of careers, we must address the set of incentives that students have for entering lower-paying careers. Forgiveness of loan repayments for students who agree to enter designated professions is one policy mechanism that has traditionally been used in this regard. Scholarships have also been used to encourage students to enter designated professions, but insofar as these scholarships must be repaid if the student does not fulfill the commitment, the net effect of a grant with a repayment is the same as a loan with a forgiveness feature.

Loan forgiveness for borrowers who chose to go into teaching was a prominent part of the initial NDSL (now Perkins) loan program, but was phased out in the 1970s, a victim of its own success or failure, depending on one's point of view. At that time there was a surfeit of teachers, and it seemed inappropriate to keep an incentive on the books that was designed to generate

2. U.S. Department of Education, *Digest of Education Statistics,* 1988.

more teachers. But the surplus of teachers was not so much a result of increases in the percentage of college students who chose teaching—a proportion that varied little over time despite the provision of loan forgiveness—as a result of the increase in the number of college graduates and a decrease in the number of school-age children. In the late 1980s the numbers of school-age children started to pick up again, teacher shortages began to reemerge, and as many as half the states passed loan forgiveness provisions for teachers. Because of its past experience, however, the federal government has not renewed its previous broad loan-forgiveness provisions.

The federal student loan programs still contain limited loan forgiveness provisions for designated types of teaching and certain kinds of public service jobs. In the Stafford loan program, for example, borrowers who teach in areas with high concentrations of low-income students or handicapped students can have their loan repayment obligations forgiven. All or part of the loan repayment is forgiven for borrowers who enter the Peace Corps, VISTA, or other designated positions. Furthermore, the federal health professional loan programs forgive borrowers who agree to practice in rural or other designated underserved areas.

The experience with loan forgiveness suggests a pattern of very limited success in meeting program objectives. By and large, the availability of loan forgiveness does not seem to motivate large numbers of students to alter their career plans. This is not all that surprising, since the amount of aid provided through loan forgiveness does not constitute a large proportion of the salary differential that led to the problem in the first place. If a student is facing a lifetime salary differential of $10,000 or $20,000 a year between career opportunities, the cancellation of $1,000 or $2,000 in annual loan repayments is probably insufficient to affect the job decision of such a student.

A disadvantage of loan forgiveness is that borrowers are identified as being eligible for aid while they are still in school, although the labor market need that led to the forgiveness provision may well change by the time the borrower is ready to take a position. This aspect of loan forgiveness is somewhat inefficient in that a benefit must be provided for all borrowers who agree to participate, including those whose income after graduation does not justify such a benefit.

If student aid programs are to be used as an incentive to get students to enter relatively low-paying jobs, it is preferable to provide the kind of low-income insurance discussed earlier in this chapter. Low-income insurance would affect only those borrowers who enter lower-income jobs or are unemployed, not those borrowers who enter lower-paying professions. Nor do borrowers have to be identified while still in school, many years before they are ready to enter the labor market. In this regard, some law schools and other professional schools that now offer low-income insurance to their graduates who choose lower-paying positions would seem to have made the right policy choice.

Proposals for a Program of National Service

Periodically over the past several decades many distinguished individuals, organizations, and commissions have proposed that a system of national service be created. These proposals have taken different forms, depending on their predominant concerns. One approach would reinstitute the military draft with a civilian alternative service component. Another would reestablish a "conservation corps" at either the federal or state level to accomplish a set of tasks related to improving the environment and other social problems. Still another would establish a program of service separate from the military draft as a means of reinstituting basic citizenship values.

The proposals also vary widely with respect to when young people would be asked or would volunteer to perform the service. Some would focus on students before they enroll in postsecondary education. Others would encourage college students to perform community service while they are enrolled or during the summer months. Still other proposals would provide incentives for college students to engage in service-related activities once they graduate or complete their education.

Many of these proposals would provide financial assistance in return for the service they provide. One approach would provide educational benefits for people who served in the Peace Corps, VISTA, or other similar programs. A related proposal would provide loan forgiveness in return for this kind of service. Some of the proposals would extend college work-study funds to students who perform designated kinds of community service either on or off campus. Still others would provide education benefits for individuals who served in their communities on the weekend, under arrangements akin to those established for the national guard.

Only one of these proposals, however, would require people to serve in order to receive student aid benefits. The Democratic Leadership Council (DLC), a group of moderate Democrats, has proposed the creation of a citizens corps, which it describes as essentially a new GI Bill that would reward civilian as well as military service to the nation. The elements of the DLC plan are reflected in legislation introduced by Senator Sam Nunn (Democrat of Georgia) and Representative Dave McCurdy (Democrat of Oklahoma) in the early days of the 101st Congress. Under this legislation, in exchange for one or two years of service at subsistence wages, members of the citizens corps would receive vouchers they could use to pay for college expenses, vocational training, or the purchase of a home. The purpose of the corps, as with most national service proposals, would be to raise civic consciousness, to meet long-deferred social and infrastructure needs, to help meet military labor force needs, and to expand opportunities for those who enter either military or civilian service.

A citizens corps would restore in a dramatic way the connection between service and student aid that existed in the GI Bill and other earlier student aid efforts. The most controversial aspect of the plan is that vouchers would replace the existing federal student aid programs of grants and loans. To receive aid, people would have to serve first in the civilian corps. The current programs of student grants would eventually be eliminated for most students while eligibility for loans would be restricted to "corps veterans." This service requirement would be waived for certain groups of students, including handicapped students and those for whom no placement was available.

Advocates of the citizens corps idea argue that making participation in the corps a precondition of aid will provide a sounder
base of public support than is now enjoyed by the existing student
aid programs. They suggest that such an arrangement would
clear up some of the most obvious problems experienced by the
current student aid programs by reversing the shift from grants
to loans and substantially reducing the costs of student loan
defaults. They also point out that the vouchers would provide
more aid to participants than the current aid programs do.

Proponents of the plan estimate that a full-blown citizens corps
would cost the federal government only several billion dollars
more than the current student aid programs, once savings from
restrictions in eligibility are taken into account. But these kinds
of costs can only be achieved if far fewer people receive aid
through the citizens corps than currently receive aid through the
student programs. More than five million people now receive
federal student aid each year—a number that would probably be
sharply reduced under the citizen corps approach. If the number
of beneficiaries is kept at current levels, the citizens corps proposal
would cost as much as $50 billion annually. Put another way,
since the amount of benefits provided to citizens corps volunteers
would be five to ten times greater than the average student aid
benefit in the current system, it would not be surprising if the
annual costs were five to ten times greater than the $9 billion in
annual federal costs for student aid, *assuming the same number
of beneficiaries.*

The controversy created by the citizens corps plan revolves
principally around the prospect that it would discriminate in a
rather marked way on the basis of a person's family income.
Students from middle- and upper-income families could avoid
service in the corps and still be able to afford a college education.
Students from lower-income families would not have such a
choice; realistically, most of them could pay for their postsecondary education only if they first participated in the corps.

This feature of the plan runs counter to several fairly well
accepted policy principles in education. The first is that students
from disadvantaged circumstances should be provided with an
equal opportunity to continue their education. Just as important,

the notion of national service has traditionally derived from the principle that participation should not be a function of income and circumstance. If we were to move away from that principle, we would in effect be returning to the situation in the nineteenth century, when the wealthy could buy a way out of (military) service while the poor could not.

One obvious way to avoid making a distinction between rich and poor students is not to insist on participation in the corps as a prerequisite for student aid. For example, the amount of aid that students receive could be greater if they participated than if they did not, while the existing student aid programs could still be maintained. Thus the citizens corps would be much closer to the GI Bill, in which the education benefits for those who served have typically been more generous than what was available through the other federal student aid programs for those who did not serve. Of course, this modification would alter the marginal cost to the government noticeably. To reduce federal costs, the new benefits could be financed in several ways, including selective cuts in the existing student aid programs, a reduction in the number of service slots, and smaller benefits for service.

Another way to prevent discrimination against poorer students is to have a system of mandatory service for rich and poor alike. A groundswell of support for mandatory service is unlikely, however, as long as military service is voluntary. The only realistic scenario in which mandatory civilian service might and should be adopted would be if it was an alternative to renewed military conscription.

Most of the recent debate over national service has centered on the citizens corps proposal. Its requirement that people serve in order to receive aid is so controversial that it will probably spell doom for the plan in the legislature. There is simply very little support for the proposal in its current form because of this requirement.

What seems likely to happen is that a federal demonstration project will be enacted that incorporates elements of at least several of the proposals now being discussed. For example, the citizens corps might be tested, although probably not with a major service requirement. Additional federal educational ben-

efits might be provided to encourage service in the Peace Corps
and VISTA, as well as in state and local programs like the
California Conservation Corps or the New York City Volunteer
Corps. Education or housing benefits might be extended to those
who perform community service on the weekends. It is also likely
that the use of college work-study for community service opportunities will be expanded. Given the size of the federal budget
deficit, however, it is unlikely that funding for this eclectic
approach to national service would exceed $500 million a year.

Chapter Four

Policy Issues
and Directions

The financing of higher education in the United States, especially since the end of the Second World War, has been marked by a high degree of creativity and experimentation in response to emerging national needs and priorities. The GI Bill was the federal government's innovative way of providing an opportunity for large numbers of returning veterans to continue their education. Programs of loan forgiveness and fellowships contained in the National Defense Education legislation represented an effort to boost enrollments in targeted fields of study, particularly in the sciences and engineering, in reaction to competition with the Soviet Union in the 1950s. What are now thought of as the traditional student aid programs of grants, loans, and work-study initially gained impetus as part of Lyndon Johnson's Great Society programs of the 1960s. The loan programs blossomed in the late 1970s to fill the growing gap between the costs of attendance and what families felt they could afford to pay.

The innovative financing mechanisms examined in this book are the 1980s policy response to perceived inadequacies in the current system of paying for college. They are an attempt to address the fact that the traditional student aid programs and family incomes have not kept pace with the rapid growth in college charges over the past decade. In this context these new approaches can reasonably be viewed as a continuation of the historical inclination of Americans to seek creative solutions when faced with major obstacles in higher education, and to experiment with new ideas to meet the changing financial needs of students and their families.

As a result of this creativity and experimentation, however, the new or repackaged mechanisms discussed here do not fit neatly into a prescribed set of categories. Nor can they easily be assessed by a single criterion, since they have been developed in response to different concerns and needs. The methods of paying for college are similar to the system of American higher education itself—both are diverse and complex.

In most respects, this characteristic of diversity is a notable strength of both the system and the means by which it is financed. But it does complicate the job of determining what should be done in the area of financing and who should do it. The decision is not simply a matter of determining whether or not to adopt a new financing plan to help students and their parents pay for college costs. But which one should it be? In making these decisions, federal, state, institutional, and private sector policymakers face at least three sets of choices:

—They must choose among various objectives recognizing that often these objectives will conflict with one another.

—They must choose among different plans, recognizing that there are opportunity costs in choosing one plan over another.

—They must choose within a given category of plans which is the best for their organization or for the set of students that they wish to serve.

Policymakers also face a broader set of choices that must be made collectively about the appropriate role of federal and state governments, educational institutions, foundations, and the private sector in the development of these various new financing plans. Which organizations or governmental entities are best suited for promoting and administering different types of plans? The discussion in this chapter attempts to bring some order out of the chaos.

Policy Objectives

The task of deciding whether to promote a new financing plan for higher education, and which one it should be, is complicated by the fact that the goals one group of participants may wish to achieve often differ from those of another.

For college students and their parents, a primary objective is to ease the burden of paying for college. They are interested in maximizing their potential choice of institutions. Because of the rapid increase in tuitions and other charges in the 1980s, many parents are also intent on reducing uncertainties about what a college education will cost when their children are ready to enroll.

For college presidents and other administrators, a primary objective is to maintain or increase the enrollments at their institutions without sacrificing the quality of the education they provide or of the applicants they admit. They are also interested in maintaining or increasing the diversity of their student bodies and in stimulating the development of proper values and ethics in their students.

For federal and state government officials, concerns will often coincide with those of either the consumers or the providers of higher education. As public officials, they want to ensure the availability of collegiate and vocational opportunities of high quality, commensurate with the range of individual abilities and needs. In response to consumer concerns, they want to restrain the growth in college charges in order to ease the financial burden placed on parents and students. They, like many college officials, want to encourage the development of ethical and moral behavior. But they must also be keenly intent on minimizing the cost to the taxpayer.

For foundation officers, corporate leaders, and others in the private sector, a primary objective is to maximize the effective use of the resources they devote to postsecondary education. Corporate officials, for example, may be motivated to invest in education to maximize the productivity of their current and future employees. Foundation heads and their staffs want to leverage their resources so that they will be of the most use in achieving the goals of their organizations, which include easing the financing burden, instilling better values, and many others.

The financing approaches discussed in this book are good examples of how the general policy objectives just described are being translated into specific programmatic responses. The wide differences in objectives are reflected in the diversity of the new financing plans now being developed. The desire to increase incentives for parents and students to save has resulted in the recent boom in savings incentives and tuition prepayment plans. The interest in ensuring adequate student credit opportunities is evidenced by the creation of less subsidized federal student loan programs as well as numerous state, institutional, and private loan efforts. The burst of enthusiasm for assured access efforts indicates the high priority that many place on increasing the participation of low-income and minority students in post-secondary education. Those who are interested in improving quality will frequently seek to do so by expanding the use of merit-based aid. Policymakers who place a high priority on the development of good citizenship and societal values will lean toward proposals that link aid to the performance of community or national service.

As with most other issues of public concern, the amount of resources available falls far short of what is needed to fulfill all the worthy objectives. Although it is tempting for policymakers to try to achieve many objectives with their limited resources, budget constraints do help to focus the debate. Policymakers interested in developing new ways to pay for college thus find themselves faced with a familiar question: which objectives are the most important and therefore deserve the greatest investment?

Potential Roles

The roles that the federal and state governments, educational institutions, and the private sector may play in the development of new financing mechanisms are varied. They include that of subsidizer, guarantor, employer, loan capitalizer, loan forgiver, and promoter or sponsor. Some of these roles entail a large infusion of funds, whereas others involve little or no financial commitment. Policymakers should obviously keep in mind the strengths and weaknesses of their organizations in deciding which are the most appropriate roles they might serve.

Subsidizer. The principal function that governments and others perform in providing student aid is to reduce the costs of attending college. These subsidies often take the form of grant assistance that lowers the net price students face. The federal government also serves as a subsidizer when it pays or forgives the interest for borrowers while they are in school and when it pays lenders a special allowance to make the rate of return on student loans competitive with other investments. Other groups such as institutions or foundations could also possibly assume this role as loan subsidizer, although in general that has not been the case.

Guarantor. An important function that an organization can perform is to act as a guarantor, which can be done in several ways. The federal government acts as a guarantor when it insulates lenders against the risk of loan defaults in the Stafford (GSL) and other federal student loan programs. Eugene Lang was, in essence, also acting as a guarantor when he told his class of students that he would pay their educational costs if they were admitted to college. Michigan and the other states that have established tuition guarantee programs are also serving in the role of guarantor by protecting students and their families against the adverse effects of increased tuitions.

Employer. Organizations also provide financial assistance to students by employing them. Available data on student employment indicate that the private sector remains the predominant employer of college students. Colleges and universities also provide employment opportunities for their students, primarily through the college work-study program. By contrast, federal and state governments usually do not directly serve as employers of college students; efforts like the California Conservation Corps are exceptions. But since federal funds provide 80 percent of the wages paid to students in the college work-study program, it could be argued that the federal government is in fact a major employer of college students. Governments and others can also involve themselves not by being employers, but by serving as locators of jobs or service opportunities, such as the State Employment Service.

Loan capitalizer. With the growth of the GSL program, banks and other private financial institutions have become the primary source of capital for student loans. By funding the Perkins loan program, the federal government also serves as a source of capital for student loans, but in a decidedly smaller way than the private sector does in GSL. State issuance of tax-exempt bonds is another

source of student loan capital. In many instances the federal
government and others can facilitate the provision of loan capital
without actually sacrificing their own funds. For example, the
federal creation of the Student Loan Marketing Association (Sallie
Mae) in 1972 and the subsequent evolution of state and private
secondary markets have helped tremendously in expanding capital without directly involving much in the way of a governmental
budgetary commitment.

Loan forgiver. A traditional role of government in student aid
has been to reduce the loan repayment obligations of students
who enter designated professions or fields of study. The National
Defense Education Act of 1958 included loan forgiveness provisions for borrowers who became teachers, and elements of this
forgiveness were incorporated into the Higher Education Act.
Although federal loan forgiveness became restricted after the
early 1970s as teacher shortages evaporated, state efforts along
this line have grown, especially in recent years as teacher
shortages reemerged. Some institutions have also initiated loan
forgiveness. A dozen or so law schools now offer some form of
loan abatement for their graduates who choose public service
careers. Foundations could also become involved by providing
financial support for such a program. Some proposals for linking
public service to student aid would provide loan forgiveness in
return for designated forms of service.

Promoter or sponsor. While making little financial commitment, organizations can perform many functions that highlight
or publicize existing or new student aid initiatives. For example,
they can promote a plan that is funded or capitalized by others.
Sometimes sponsorship involves lending an organizational or
individual imprimatur through board memberships or other
affiliations. In other instances new plans can be sponsored or
promoted through in-kind contributions for space or other needs.
Another important form of sponsorship entails making sure that
adequate and accurate information is available on student aid
opportunities. For example, the Massachusetts Higher Education
Assistance Corporation has greatly expanded consumer knowl-
edge and understanding of financing opportunities at relatively

low cost through its sponsorship of an information center at the Boston Public Library.

Issues for Policymakers

The task of deciding whether to adopt any of the new financing plans discussed in this report and other plans that have not yet emerged will fall on a large number and variety of policymakers, including federal legislators, their staffs, and officials in the federal executive branch; governors, state legislators, and their staffs; college presidents and institutional finance officers; foundation heads and their representatives; and employers and other decisionmakers in the private sector. These policymakers will have to deal with many difficult questions as they think about how a college education should be financed in the future, decide on the merits of alternative financing approaches, or choose among different plans. They will need to identify the groups of students that will receive the benefits, the risks entailed for the various participants, the approaches that are likely to be most effective in meeting policy goals, the educational and administrative considerations, and the extent to which the new or repackaged ideas fit into the existing system of college financing.

Which students will receive the benefits provided under the plan? Does the plan provide a benefit to the consumer? Is the plan better than what is already available? Is the plan a good deal for the students or their parents? If so, who pays for the benefits? Are the subsidies that are provided targeted on the neediest students? If funds are not targeted, are they likely to detract from student aid programs that are targeted?

Does the plan entail new risks and contingent liabilities? Does the plan involve a future financial commitment that is difficult to estimate or predict? Who assumes that commitment? Are financial risks transferred from one party to another? Who bears this shifting of risks?

How effective is the plan in closing the gap between resources and costs? Are the incentives that are provided likely to change student or family behavior in a desirable way? Does the plan help the student meet all costs of attendance, or are just tuition costs covered? Does the plan address gaps in coverage in the existing student aid programs?

What educational or administrative considerations are attached to the plan? Does the plan affect students' ability to pick the best institution for them? Is choice of institution restricted in the plan? Is the plan easy to understand, so that a broad range of students and families will be able to participate? Is the plan complex and therefore difficult to administer?

How well does the plan fit into the existing financing arrangements? Would this plan complement and supplement what is already being done? Or would it replace existing financing mechanisms? To what extent should these innovative plans replace the traditional financing mechanisms? Or would it be better to layer them onto the existing system?

Sorting Out Roles and Responsibilities for New Financing Approaches

The remainder of this chapter attempts to address these questions. The discussion focuses on the principal types of the financing mechanisms that have been described: savings and tuition guarantee plans, alternative loan programs, assured access strategies, merit-based aid, and proposals that would link student aid with service. This section draws heavily on the discussions that occurred at the Brookings forum on new college financing mechanisms held in June 1988.

Savings and Tuition Guarantee Plans

The fundamental policy issue regarding the many college savings incentives that have emerged in recent years is whether they will, in fact, result in additional savings. The answer to this question appears to be, probably not much. The incentives provided through these plans may well change the mix of assets that parents and students use to save for college, but altering the overall rate of saving would require providing a much larger financial incentive than the modest ones being offered in the savings and tuition guarantee plans developed thus far. In addition, the subsidies provided through most savings incentive and tuition guarantee plans will normally accrue to wealthier families because they are the ones who have the resources to save. This skewed distribution of benefits argues heavily against any plan that entails large subsidies.

Even without large incentives to save and even though the subsidies will go mostly to wealthier families, a modest governmental commitment to encourage savings for college may nonetheless be worthwhile for several related reasons. First, it would serve as a signal that it is a good idea for parents to save for their children's education rather than be caught unprepared for the bill. Moreover, to the extent that parents do save, their need for financial aid will be diminished, and this will relieve at least some of the political pressure for increased funding of the student aid programs. Along the same lines, if middle-class families save more as a result of these savings plans, some funds may be freed up for the neediest students whose families are unable to save. This was referred to at the forum as a trickle-down theory of college finance. Finally, to the extent that equity is a concern, there are ways to reduce the share of benefits going to well-to-do families, although these restrictions typically add to the complexity of the plan.

Despite the flurry of state and federal governmental activity in recent years to develop savings incentives, private financial institutions remain the primary providers of college savings funds through the variety of financial instruments they offer. This reliance on the private sector should continue for at least two reasons. First, the private sector has the most expertise and experience in developing and marketing mutual funds, tax-exempt financing, zero-coupon bonds, and the other financial instruments that readily lend themselves for use in saving for college. It is probably better to draw upon this private sector experience than to have governments or colleges try to develop their own expertise in this area. Second, for the middle- and

upper-income families who are most likely to participate in and
benefit from savings and tuition guarantee programs, private
plans with little or no government subsidy remain the most
appropriate savings vehicle. The general absence of government
subsidies in these savings programs means that aid resources
can be targeted on lower-income students.

It follows that the primary role of the federal government in
the area of savings should be that of a promoter and a sponsor
rather than a subsidizer. The federal government should encourage families to begin saving earlier for college and should provide
information on savings opportunities that exist nationwide. But
the federal budgetary commitment to college savings incentives
should be minimized; instead, federal funds should be targeted
on the neediest students.

To improve the equity of the provision that exempts from
taxation interest on U.S. savings bonds, it could be revised into
a spending provision in which the interest paid on the bonds
would be higher (and taxed) if used for college expenses. Such a
subsidy would be more valuable to students from lower-income
families than a tax exemption of similar size would be. And there
would be one less tax loophole. It would also be worthwhile to
reconsider the current tax treatment of gifts to children so that
saving for college is encouraged for younger children, rather than
discouraged, as is now the case.

The federal and state governments, in concert with the colleges,
could also promote more savings by altering the rules that are
now used to calculate the amount of expected family contribution
to be made from parental and student savings. Lower expectations
of contributions from savings could serve as an incentive for
families to save more for college. But it is not clear that the
current rules are sufficiently onerous to stimulate parents to
draw down or alter the mix of assets they hold. Moreover, changing
these rules would result in greater aid eligibility for students
from middle- and upper-income families, which runs counter to
the principle of targeting aid dollars to the neediest students.

Thus far the states have been the most active participants in
establishing savings and tuition guarantee plans. By the end of

1989 more than half of them had passed legislation that either provides tuition guarantees or creates incentives for college savings. Most of the states that have acted have opted for savings incentives over tuition guarantees. This is a trend in the right direction, since most states seem to be hesitant about committing themselves to the possibility of large contingent liabilities and are worried about the potential adverse effects of tuition guarantees.

Another possible role for the states that has not yet emerged is to provide small subsidies for federal, institutional, or private savings plans. For example, it would be reasonable for states to supplement the return on the federal savings bonds used to pay for college expenses. These subsidies should be limited to students from low- and moderate-income families. To meet this objective, the additional interest payments could be targeted on students who are eligible for state grant assistance. The states, like the federal government, can also promote or sponsor nongovernmental savings plans without a commitment of taxpayer dollars.

The role of colleges and universities in the development of savings plans has been minimal and should continue to be so. They typically have neither the resources nor the expertise to justify an expanded role in this area. Moreover, to the extent that the benefits of such a plan would be limited to the institution(s) that participated in its development, choice would be restricted rather than expanded. The one reasonable function for institutions might be for consortia of them to act as sponsors or promoters of plans to encourage more savings for college, regardless of which college or university a student chose to attend.

Overall, it is not realistic to expect that savings will or should assume a substantially larger role in the financing of postsecondary education. The amount of subsidies needed to produce such additional savings would be large and probably not cost-effective. But modest subsidies and heavier promotion of savings plans could have the beneficial effects of increasing moderately the amount saved and relieving some of the pressure on the student aid programs by reducing the financial need of some middle-class families.

Alternative Loan Programs

The recurrent concerns expressed about the growing imbalance of loans versus grants suggest that student loans should be deemphasized and grants should be raised to a higher priority. But the amount of funds needed to increase grants sufficiently to redress the current imbalance is so large that it is not realistic to expect this to happen in the near future. Moreover, the growing costs of college attendance preclude the possibility of simply slipping back to the "good old days" when loans played a minor role in the financing of higher education. It would be more realistic to examine how the growth in loans might be restrained, how the costs of loans might be minimized, and how repayment burdens might be made more manageable.

The federal government, by virtue of its long involvement and substantial investment in the Stafford program, is likely to continue to maintain its role of guaranteeing private sector loans to both students and their parents. There seems to be general agreement that the federal government should provide the assurance of repayment to lenders that students without adequate physical capital cannot. It is not as obvious, however, that the current guarantee arrangement is the most appropriate one. The federal government pays almost all the costs associated with defaults, since there is very little risk sharing in the current program. This could be modified by having the origination fee that students currently pay in the Stafford program changed into a default fee, which would offset at least in part the federal costs of defaults. In addition, some degree of risk sharing should be required of lenders and institutions that participate in the program, while the federal government would continue to serve as the backup guarantor. In effect, it would be better if the federal role was more that of an insurer, in which the premiums paid by participants were used to pay default costs, than that of a full guarantor.

Agreement that the federal government should continue to act in some capacity as a loan guarantor does not mean that its other major role in loans—that of subsidizer—should also be maintained in its current form. The high degree of subsidy in the Stafford program has been a significant factor in the growth of student loans, as students and their families find these loans to be an attractive financing mechanism. It can also reasonably be argued that the costs of paying for these interest subsidies have served as an obstacle to greater funding of the student grant programs. Furthermore, the high degree of subsidy makes it more difficult for states, institutions, and the private sector to establish competitive alternative loan programs. These factors argue for a reexamination of how much subsidy is provided, and also for greater use of the PLUS and SLS programs because they entail substantially lower federal costs than GSL.

The federal government might also investigate extending its role as a source of loan capital. The decision in 1965 to use private loan capital for the GSL program was motivated by a set of factors that may not be as relevant today. The use of federal capital, whether in the form of direct appropriations or borrowing, could entail smaller federal costs than those currently paid in the program because the subsidy to private lenders to encourage their participation could be sharply reduced or entirely avoided.

Alternative repayment arrangements should also be investigated at the federal level. Any large-scale increase in the use of loans to finance postsecondary education should be accompanied by a system of income-contingent repayments so that student borrowers will be able to manage their larger repayment obligations. The notion of repaying through the payroll tax mechanism is particularly attractive because it would avert many of the problems that can arise under an income tax-based system of repayment.

Current levels of borrowing probably do not justify introducing a full-scale income-contingent approach. Most borrowers do not currently find repayment a problem and should not be asked to subsidize those borrowers who are having difficulty. Instead, concerns about current borrowing levels and defaults should be addressed through a program of low-income insurance, which could be instituted under the current system to provide repayment relief and to lower defaults for those borrowers whose repayment obligations exceed a reasonable proportion of their incomes once they complete their education.

The federal predominance in student loans in the past has led to a subsidiary role for states, institutions, and the private sector, since the degree of federal subsidy makes for an uneven playing field. But concerns over the size of the federal budget deficit and a growing conviction that the federal loan programs require some major adjustment may open the door for greater nonfederal involvement in student loans. That is to say, states, institutions, or foundations could directly provide loan capital. But the resources of these organizations are constrained and could not generate adequate capital levels. It would seem more appropriate for them to concentrate, instead, on providing subsidies on privately financed loans, in many cases substituting for what the federal government has previously provided. For example, institutions or foundations could pay all or a portion of the in-school interest for needy borrowers who find that they cannot participate in the federally subsidized programs, or for whom current federal loan limits are insufficient to meet their borrowing needs. Another reasonable role for states, institutions, or foundations would be to provide full or partial loan forgiveness for students who enter designated professions or who opt for public service over more lucrative private endeavors.

Any expansion of nonfederal loans should be accompanied by a coordination effort which ensures that borrowers can consolidate the repayments of the loans they borrow under different programs. Otherwise, the complexity and confusion arising out of multiple loan programs will negate the benefits of opening up alternative sources of capital and subsidies. It would be good public policy to institute better coordination of loan repayments among different programs now, even without any other change in the student loan structure.

Assured Access Strategies

As with savings incentives, it is not realistic to expect assured access efforts to rearrange how higher education is financed in this country. But Eugene Lang's impromptu experiment, and other, less publicized efforts attest to the potential for improving the participation of disadvantaged students through assured access strategies. These efforts also reinforce the notion that to be successful, assured access must be multifaceted—and must involve not just money, but hope, support, and the personal touch.

Under Eugene Lang's leadership, the philanthropic sector has assumed a principal role in the development of assured access efforts across this country. This leadership role is consistent with a philosophy of philanthropy that seeks to fill the gaps in the coverage provided by governments. In this instance, government aid has not been sufficient to provide the neediest students with access to a wide range of postsecondary options. There has also been a lack of coordination between aid and support services efforts, and most students are not aware of aid availability early enough in the high school years to affect student choices. Philanthropy has stepped into this breach, as evidenced by the many donors willing to establish assured access programs.

But assuring disadvantaged youth that they will have full access to a broad range of postsecondary education exceeds the financial capacity of the philanthropic sector. At a minimum, several billion dollars each year would be required to meet that collective need. At present, all philanthropic efforts along this line entail several million dollars annually. Moreover, the random quality of individual philanthropists adopting classes of students does not represent a particularly reassuring policy response. Some greater institutionalization of the concept is desirable.

Although a handful of colleges and universities have attempted to provide assured access to their institutions, this method is also not likely to be successful. Institutions cannot raise the necessary level of funds without greatly increasing the tuitions they charge to their unaided students, a strategy that already is starting to fray at the edges. And colleges and universities acting individually obviously cannot provide a range of choice of institutions. Consortia of institutions would provide greater choice, but it would still be limited.

The states would appear to be the most likely candidate for the successful adoption of a complete assured access strategy. They are less removed from the students than the federal government but have greater resources than foundations or the institutions themselves. They also control the tuitions charged in the public sector, which remain the primary tool for providing access to higher education in the United States. Finally, it is usually the aid that a state or institution provides that serves as the final piece of the puzzle in determining the size of a student's aid package. These marginal dollars often are critical in a student's decision where to go to college.

The federal government, short of a massive funding increase for Pell grants, cannot provide assured access. Nor is it clear that greater funding of student aid is the answer. The Lang experiment demonstrates that successfully providing access to college for disadvantaged students is more than a matter of money. Even with large increases in Pell grant funding, it is not apparent that access would be assured without the other critical components in the Lang approach: earlier awareness of aid eligibility and better support services.

One potential role for the federal government, however, is to serve as the "guarantor" of aid early in a student's high school years. Under the current system, students and their families do not know whether they will be eligible for aid until the spring before they are ready to enroll; many do not know until shortly before they matriculate. What the federal government could do is to establish a process in which eligibility for aid is determined for economically disadvantaged students as early as the seventh or ninth grade. Aid eligibility could be established by students submitting an application, or by virtue of their being eligible for some other form of public assistance such as welfare or the school lunch program. Participation in the school lunch program was the route for student eligibility in the original formulation of the New York Liberty scholarship legislation, although it was eventually eliminated in the legislative process.

In this way, students would be assured that they would be eligible for the full measure of federal aid when and if they are admitted to a postsecondary education program. This assurance would not increase federal costs very much, in that available data indicate that the economic circumstances of disadvantaged youth do not change much over time. The vast majority of students deemed eligible for full federal aid in the seventh or ninth grade will also be fully eligible when they reach college age.

The federal government can also contribute to the goal of assured access by strengthening its commitment to the TRIO programs that provide student support services. This enhanced commitment should take at least two forms. First, more funding is necessary so that a higher proportion of eligible students can receive this important kind of assistance. It could reasonably be argued that TRIO funding should increase faster than funding for student aid to increase the effectiveness of the student aid dollars. Second, the TRIO funding formula should be revised so that federal funds are not as focused as they are now on institutions with established programs of support services. A formula that, instead, provided matching funds to those institutions with high concentrations of disadvantaged students and which demonstrated a willingness to commit more of their own funds to these efforts might be more effective in increasing the participation of "at-risk" students. Federal funds would then "reward" those institutions that made the effort to enroll and, more important, to retain the most economically disadvantaged students.

The main obligation of providing greater participation for disadvantaged students in postsecondary education should, however, continue to rest with the colleges and universities. Philanthropic, state, and federal efforts can only provide the funds and some direction about their use. Whether a student actually enrolls and completes a postsecondary educational program depends ultimately on the commitment of the institution at which he or she enrolls. With or without government incentives and funds, colleges and universities must increase the support services they provide to improve both the postsecondary participation and retention rates of economically disadvantaged students.

Providing Merit-Based Aid

In the thirty-five years since the adoption of the needs analysis principles and system, merit-based aid has gone from being the predominant to the subsidiary form of financial assistance for undergraduates. During the same time it has remained the principal source of aid for doctoral students. This is an appropriate set of priorities if the goal of equal educational opportunity is ever to be achieved. Nonetheless, some expansion in the use of merit-based aid at the undergraduate level may be justified at this time to reinforce the priority attached to improving quality by rewarding students for their academic and other achievements. In particular, this expansion in merit-based aid can be justified if it is combined with the principle of determining the amount of aid that a student receives on the basis of financial need.

It seems reasonable that educational institutions should continue to be the primary providers of the merit-based aid that is available. They are in the best position to compare the qualifications of applicants and to decide which of their students might benefit most from a higher proportion of grants or an infusion of additional aid over and above need-based assistance. At the same time, institutions should not be encouraged to abandon or reverse the needs analysis principles that have evolved over the past three decades. It is unfortunate that many institutions appear to be using merit-based criteria to award a growing share of their own aid as a means of competing for students.

The overwhelming proportion of aid that the federal government provides or guarantees for undergraduates should continue to be based on financial need. Without such a federal commitment, the objective of improving participation in postsecondary education would be meaningless. At the same time, federal aid to graduate school students in the form of fellowships and assistantships should continue primarily on a merit basis. If the federal government wishes to place a higher priority on the issue of quality, it could establish or expand programs of merit-based undergraduate aid in which high achievers were recognized for their accomplishments, but funds were awarded on the basis of financial need. The most obvious way to do this is to give nominal awards to people with no financial need, while providing much larger awards to needy students, as determined by the standards that apply in the need-based programs, similar to many private national merit programs.

The proliferation of small merit-based aid programs in the states is also not a positive policy trend: it complicates the application process for students, parents, and aid administrators. More important, it reduces the focus on equal opportunity at the state level if a higher proportion of state dollars are provided on a basis other than financial need. Some consolidation of these smaller programs would prove helpful, as would the introduction of a need basis in the determination of how much merit-based aid students should receive.

Linking Community Service with Student Aid

The advantages of linking student aid with service are that it encourages young Americans to become more involved in voluntary activities, teaches them to perform worthwhile services that are now not being accomplished, creates a reasonable alternative to military service, and changes the system of financing postsecondary education in this country. Among these objectives, using national service as a means of altering the system of postsecondary educational finance ranks at the bottom. The amount of funds that reasonably could be released for service constitutes a small share of the overall bill for college costs. Moreover, none of the current proposals for national service effectively address the needs of the students who do not perform service, who under any conceivable service plan would still constitute the vast majority of college students. It is, therefore, more reasonable to view the service proposals as having only a peripheral effect on future financing patterns in postsecondary education.

After a gestation period spanning several decades, the idea of encouraging young Americans to increase the voluntary service they perform has moved to the front burner of national issues. The spark for this resurgence has been the proposal by the Democratic Leadership Council and the related Nunn-McCurdy legislation to create a citizens corps of high school graduates to provide much-needed service in the fields of health care, education, environment, and other areas. The debate over the citizens corps proposal has overshadowed the rapid grass roots growth of community service projects on campuses and in communities across the country. The debate over this one proposal has also obscured the dozens of other federal legislative proposals that have been introduced to encourage greater voluntary service.

The great diversity in existing service programs and in the legislative proposals for expansion make it difficult to determine the proper role of various organizations in encouraging more service. It might therefore be more appropriate for this discussion to enumerate several principles that policymakers could use to guide them in choosing among the many alternatives that already exist, as well as what else may be brought forward.

A first principle is that the locus of volunteer activity should continue to be at the state, local, or institutional level and should not be shifted to the federal government. The whole notion of community service is based on the premise that it is something that people do voluntarily and not through governmental coercion or incentives. This suggests the federal role should be to promote or sponsor, and possibly to subsidize, in pushing forward the concept of service, but not to act as the primary employer or enforcer. It seems inappropriate to take what has largely been a philanthropic or institutional activity and move it into the federal arena.

Second, service should be encouraged at different times of the life cycle. It should not be restricted to a particular time, such as right after high school graduation, or while students are enrolled in college, or once a student has graduated from college. Nor should it be restricted to just students; service programs should also seek to involve people in the work force and those in retirement. This would suggest that some of the bills now being considered might be combined so that benefits were provided for service that is performed at different times of the life cycle.

Third, service should not be a prerequisite for receiving student aid. Requiring someone to serve in order to receive aid seems the antitheses of the notion of "voluntary" service. It might be more appropriate to provide greater benefits for those students who perform service than for those who do not. This would be similar to the situation for Vietnam era veterans whose GI Bill educational benefits exceeded the amount of aid that nonveterans could receive through the student aid programs.

If service is required to receive aid, this should only be done within a system of mandatory service. Under such an approach, students from all income levels, not just the poor, would have to serve. The rich would not be able to avoid service and instead use their family resources to pay for college while the disadvantaged students were forced to serve in order to pay for their college costs.

These principles lead to a concept in which service based in the community remains the locus of volunteer activity. The federal and state governments could encourage such service by providing subsidies for the local providers or by enhancing the educational benefits that students receive in exchange for the service they have performed. It is reasonable to expect that students who perform service would receive more aid than students who do not, but that nonservers should still be eligible for aid. Subsidies and benefits should not be focused on any one aspect of the life cycle but should apply to a range of activities covering the period right after high school, during the college years, and after a student completes his or her education. Finally, to maximize the effective use of resources, federal and state funds should be provided on a matching basis that would ensure the continued effort and expenditure of funds by the organizations that sponsor such activities.

Merging New Financing Mechanisms

One of the themes that emerged at the Brookings discussion was the potential for merging aspects of two or more of the plans discussed in this book in ways that will increase the overall benefits to be obtained. Several combinations are possible: (1) parents could be allowed to borrow on the basis of how much they have saved for their children's education, (2) assured access efforts could be used as an outlet for service, and (3) trade-offs could be provided between loans and service.

Combining Loans with Savings

One possibility for combining elements of different financing plans would be to allow parents or students to borrow on the basis of how much they have saved to meet college expenses. The difficulty of predicting how much college will cost when the student is ready to enroll is one of the major concerns about the various savings plans that have been developed. In addition, the large variation in costs among institutions complicates the job of estimating the level of costs that a particular student will face—it depends on what institution he or she attends.

These difficulties in predicting future college costs for an individual student suggest that parents should not begin with the premise that they are going to save the full amount that they will need to send their children to college. Moreover, saving the full amount would essentially entail saving as much as what a college costs today and then hoping that the investment return keeps up with increases in tuition. For most families, therefore, saving the entire bill is not a realistic goal. For these reasons, families should be encouraged to put away something for college without trying to predict exactly how much they will need many years in the future.

When the amount saved is not enough to pay the total bill, it makes great sense to provide an option in which parents or students could borrow using the amount saved as partial loan collateral. Under such an arrangement, loans could be used to make up for the unpredictable difference between the amount that has been saved and how much the college selected will actually cost. Using the savings as collateral would help keep the interest rate charged lower than what would be charged for a less secured loan. Some private sector organizations now offer such a borrowing option, but it accounts for a very small fraction of current student loan volume.

It is also possible to combine loans with savings by using the amount that one group of parents and students saves as the source of capital for loans for another group of students and families. This kind of arrangement could in effect close the college financing cycle between generations: what one generation of parents saved for their younger children would be used to lend to current students and their parents. If repayment terms are kept to ten or fifteen years, then these loan repayments will be available with interest to be recouped as savings when the young children reach college age. This is essentially what is happening at the handful of campus credit unions that now use the savings from students as the source of loan capital for other students. This concept bears further examination and experimentation.

Savings could also effectively be linked with loans in how the two efforts are funded. One source of funding for savings incentives, for example, could be reduced interest subsidies on loans made to middle-income students so that there might be no overall increase in government financial commitment to students. Instead, the additional return on college savings would be paid through higher interest costs on student borrowing, thus providing an incentive to save rather than borrow.

Helping to Assure Access through Service Opportunities

One of the issues surrounding national service proposals is how much service would actually be provided. Estimates vary widely on the amount of work that could be accomplished in education, health care, environment, and other areas that have been suggested as appropriate for this type of service. Some observers have questioned whether enough opportunities for constructive projects exist to justify such an effort.

One type of service that seems particularly well suited to high school graduates or students currently enrolled in college is to be tutors or mentors in assured access efforts. If the concept of assured access really gets off the ground, the demand for people to serve in these capacities will grow rapidly and could require many thousands of participants.

Another group that could perform these functions well would be retired people who wish to put back into the community what they had received over the years. The citizens corps proposal, for example, includes provisions that encourage service by retired persons who would receive stipends (but not education or housing benefits) under the plan. Serving as mentors or tutors in assured access efforts would certainly seem to be an appropriate role for these older people.

Trading Off Loans and Service

The most controversial aspect of the citizens corps proposal is the notion that prospective college students would have to perform service to qualify for student aid. This provision is what has raised concerns that students from disadvantaged backgrounds would have to serve in order to be able to pay for college, while middle- and upper-income students could use family resources without being required to serve. Of special concern is the aspect of the proposal that would cut off federal grant assistance to students who did not perform service. Grants remain the primary student aid tool for providing access, much more so than loans, which are often viewed with suspicion by economically disadvantaged students.

Rather than create a tension between grants and service, as would occur under the citizens corps proposal, an alternative would be to establish a trade-off between loans and service. Such a trade-off might be accomplished in two ways. First, students could be provided with an opportunity to choose between service and borrowing in order to pay all or part of their costs of attendance. Let's say a student had $6,000 in family or grant resources available to attend an institution that costs $10,000 in tuition, room, board, and related expenses. Under a system that allows for trade-offs between service and loans, that student could choose to borrow $4,000, to do service before enrolling or while enrolled that netted $4,000 in aid, or to do some of both. Such a choice would allow students to reduce what would otherwise be their loan burden, thus addressing concerns about the growing reliance on loans as the primary form of student aid.

The other possible trade-off between loans and service is in the way that loan and service programs are funded. Reforms in student loans that reduce governmental default costs or interest subsidies might be used to pay for the provision of service opportunities. In such a system, restrictions in federal loan subsidies would not only create a more level playing field between different types of loans, but would also make borrowing a less attractive option and might serve to convince students to do service rather than borrow.

Conclusions

The preceding discussion on roles and responsibilities leads to some conclusions about which of the new financing mechanisms discussed in this book should be emphasized and how they should fit into the existing system of postsecondary educational finance. A reasonable amount of consensus might be reached if the proposed package included the following items:

—The creation of federal and state savings incentives that are not heavily subsidized, are not tied to guarantees of future tuition levels, and are built on private sector mechanisms.

—Reduced use of loans by lower-income students combined with a program of low-income insurance for students whose debt service exceeds their ability to repay, and possibly more systematic income-contingent repayments.

—Lowered federal student loan costs achieved through reduced interest subsidies of loans for middle-income students and additional default-prevention measures.

—Notification of Pell grant eligibility early in the high school or even junior high school years, coupled with greater targeting of aid on the neediest students and some expansion in program funding.

—Substantial expansion of mentoring and support services through philanthropic efforts and government matching programs to help ensure access to a broad range of postsecondary education for very disadvantaged students.

—Experimentation with programs in which people who perform community service at different points in their lifetimes would receive larger educational benefits than those who do not serve.

—The merging of two or more different plans, such as those that allow students and parents to borrow on the basis of how much they have saved, reward mentoring and support services in assured access efforts, and allow students to trade off between service and loans.

This package of new financing initiatives could be implemented at relatively little additional governmental cost if the expansion of grants, support services, savings incentives, and service benefits were paid for largely through the reduction in loan subsidies and defaults. Such a set of changes would not represent a revolution in how postsecondary education is financed in this country. But it would put the system on a much firmer footing to meet the challenges awaiting it in the 1990s and beyond.

Index